Out of the Ark

Out of the Ark

Rosalind Allan

HODDER AND STOUGHTON
LONDON SYDNEY AUCKLAND TORONTO

All Biblical quotations are from the
Good News Bible unless otherwise stated.

British Library Cataloguing in Publication Data

Allan, Rosalind
   Out of the ark. — (Hodder Christian
   paperbacks)
   1. Christian life
   I. Title
   248.4   BV4501.2

ISBN 0-340-39823-X

*Hodder and Stoughton Editorial Office: 47 Bedford Square, London
WC1B 3DP*

For

Penelope Jane,
aged 2¾ years

THANK YOU, GOD

Contents

Foreword

For the sake of confidentiality and to avoid confusion, some of the names have been changed in this book, but otherwise I have tried to tell it just as it happened.

I have been helped by various friends who have read and commented on part or all of the manuscript. These include Hazel Nichols, Margaret Bailey, Bryan Nicholls and Richard Miller. My heartfelt thanks go to Maureen Down for typing the manuscript in triplicate and to Martin Down for reading it, being rude about it, making me rewrite it and, above all, encouraging me to go on.

I also offer apologies to Hugh, Juliet, Rupert and Bridget, my own loving family, who have suffered long while Mum was doing it.

1. Penelope

ALLAN, on 19th May, 1966 at Gulson Hospital, Coventry, to Rosalind (née Lake) and Hugh Allan, a daughter, Penelope Jane.

Rosy-cheeked, with jet black hair and robust cry whenever hungry – the nurses said she was perfect. The grandparents doted, the cards and flowers arrived and Hugh, the proud father, made sure at last that all his friends could share his joy. He had stood or sat or snoozed beside three nights and four days of labour, marking the occasional school examination question: "'Caesar was from his mother's womb untimely ripped.' Comment."

At this point no one knew why Penelope too had been born by emergency Caesarian section; they no longer cared. Suffice it that she was alive, boisterous and beautiful. It was not until more than two years later that anyone suspected that there was anything wrong and began to question. By that time a massive fire in the office building where they were stored had destroyed all relevant records.

We were a conventional enough Coventry nuclear family in the making: two parents and one child, so far, living in a modern block of flats "ideal for first homes".

Admittedly I felt strange in such an environment. Born in High Barnet, I knew and disliked the hustle and strife of London. Yet the Kentish countryside where I grew up, and of whose beauty and simplicity I was inordinately proud, had left me strangely yearning for the vigour and challenge of city life. As a teenager, I had had many hours to think in the silence and remoteness of our house among the Kentish orchards. There was time to sit in my sloping-ceilinged bedroom at the very end of the house and listen to the soughing of the wind in the poplars outside; to wonder at the many dramatic and intimate pieces of village news which spiced conversation in the shop; to be awed at the swiftness of both birth and death; to read and reread Browning and Thomas Hardy and to realise that perhaps I was created for a purpose.

Each Sunday our family would show up at church, but there rarely seemed any life-changing connection between what we read and said there and what went on in village life.

"Stir up, we beseech thee, O Lord, the wills of thy faithful people . . ." combined instantaneously with discreet panic in the pews as my mother realised that by Stir Up Sunday the Christmas puddings should have been made. In the choir stalls my sober-faced father would shift slightly towards a fellow bass and pass the Melloids to clear everyone's throats for the anthem, the spare spectacles to anyone who had lost his place, or the peppermints to sort out digestions prior to Sunday lunch.

We none of us wanted our wills stirred up otherwise.

Thirteen: the age for confirmation. Two or three of us turned up weekly at the vicarage and chatted about village life, even about witches. We read through the catechism and claimed that its antique wording was clear enough not to have to be discussed further. Then there was the grand build-up to the ceremony in Canterbury Cathedral. We knew that now our hearts were due to be kindled afresh with the sacred flame of the Holy Spirit in the glorious setting of the Mother Church of all the churches in England.

White-robed and white-veiled we were processed . . . and came home. Nothing whatsoever had happened, or so I thought.

"Defend, O Lord, this thy child . . .", a text given by a retired missionary and duly pinned at the head of my bed, was all I had to show for My Experience! Gradually it dawned on me that I might have been deemed eternally excluded from the heavenly places. My father on earth had been a city banker. My earlier memories of him were of a gaunt-faced, dark-suited, harassed man who, upon his return at my bedtime, would enquire about the day. If my sins were too many, it was only just that he should administer the walking-stick. My Heavenly Father was probably the same, only worse – and certainly very just. Now, after my confirmation, I knelt and for the first time veritably battered at the gates of heaven, pleading with him not ultimately to reject me. A God of Wrath and Judgment I knew he was. But did he not have any love? My earthly father certainly had. All my life the smell of rough tweed had signified that other side of his nature – dependability, relaxed humorous wisdom, and toughness. Now I began to talk with my God as a homely, reassuring and totally understanding Heavenly Father. It didn't really matter that I felt so inadequate and insignificant, kneeling there by my bed. Slowly I became aware of a presence; someone was trying to get me to understand something. The blank blackness cleared, a tremendous light burst forth and a voice that was genuinely loving said,

"Whom shall I send and who will go for me?"

I was awestruck and could not respond. He surely could not be commanding, or even inviting *me*? Deep inside me, I knew that it was so. I have never forgotten that call.

But afterwards the sceptic within me mocked, and said this was the fantasising of a romantic teenager. The one fact I now confirm was that I knew I was accepted and even, perhaps, loved.

Later, having graduated and trained as a teacher, I taught for two or three years. There were many times when the practice of "religion" seemed a dry duty, but the sight of a foal finding its feet or a duck doing "up-tails-all" indicated that the Lord relished life, chuckled at my own idiosyncrasies, and I yearned to learn how to love him.

In fact he gave me this chance, soon after I graduated, to serve him more directly. An invitation arrived, offering me a job lecturing in the University of Tokyo. But I replied that I was already committed to other work. I omitted to say, first, that I was terrified of earthquakes, and, second, that I did not want to go all alone as a tall English girl amid a swarm of even younger, small Japanese students of whose language and ways I was ignorant and wary. I had been made fully aware of my duty to share the Gospel, but this was too much when all sorts of safe and exciting new prospects stretched before me in England. It is curious that I assumed that any uncomfortable, ascetic work must be an "offer from the Lord", and anything delightful was probably just "me"!

However, the performance of my duty as a Christian did assume very dry proportions indeed in my relationship with John. I had met him in some musical context at my parents' home and we had become good friends. We shared the same kind of jokes, enjoyed playing together in local chamber groups and orchestras, loved the same kind of books, sport and music, and shared many spiritual insights. John had such zest for life that he introduced me not only to Bach's coffee cantata but also to the thrills of bike-scrambling. When John asked me to marry him we had to face the fact that he did not share my belief in Jesus as Lord and Saviour and was determined to rear any children of the marriage in his religion.

We shared all that we held most dear in these matters and he became willing to find out why Jesus Christ came first in my thinking. All my explanations fell on deaf ears, despite the fact that John was keen to hear. He just could not understand what seemed to him so antiquarian, hide-bound and negative, in contrast to his own Christian Science. In desperation I wrote to the vicar of the church I had attended as a student, admitting my folly in falling in love with a non-believer and begging him to spare time to interview John, who had now become what that clergyman should be glad to call "a seeker".

The letter I received in reply was an embarrassment. Not only did I receive the expected reprimand, but also there was a lengthy, unloving diatribe against John and all he stood for. John asked to see the letter, hoping quite openly to receive enlightenment ... Very soon after that, we both knew our engagement could not continue.

I had begun teaching in girls' public schools. Now the girls I taught had seen and adored my engagement ring, knew I was leaving the school, presumably to be married, and gave me loving tokens of their approval of the romance: a breakfast-for-two set, table linen and numerous home-made gifts. One of my Cambridge contemporaries, teaching at the same school, became engaged at the same time as my engagement terminated. I had to stand in Assembly with her and my own radiantly romantic class, bellowing out with all the conviction I could muster, "Now thank we all our God." I tried to mean it.

It was during this time of teaching that I realised just how deprived and destitute of consolation were many of the girls who had become boarders because their homes and hearts were broken. But now I was not prepared to do much to help them. My own broken engagement was causing me to move on to a new job at Coventry Cathedral, as Education Officer. There were plenty of encounters now, with people from overseas, mostly students, frequently from Africa, and I had it firmly drummed into me by them that Britain itself was fast becoming the neediest mission-field of them all.

It was while I was at Coventry that I met and married Hugh, a schoolmaster in the city, and, with our lively new baby Penelope the whole world seemed to be our oyster.

Several observers from the United States prowled around my activities at the Cathedral as Education Officer. One evening when Hugh and I were making supper together the telephone rang. Hugh answered it, but in a frustrating way refused to signal who was telephoning. He was listening *very* carefully. The call was transatlantic. We were being invited by a headmaster who had met us in Coventry to come to his school in Washington, D.C. So off we went, to spend the first two years of Penelope's life in the politically seething, yet gracious whirl of the District of Columbia. The vocabulary of the baby routine became Americanised, with nappies becoming diapers, bottle teats nipples, and temperatures fevers. We made friends in the embassies, among the black people and in the drug store.

Penelope was our family's chief ambassador. Sturdy and game for anything, she could make friends even with the driver of the car behind us in a traffic jam, merely by a friendly wave and an enquiring twinkle from her big blue eyes. Neither she nor the driver knew that in my rear-view mirror I could see his smile break out.

Her greatest talent, from the time when she could sit in her high-chair and command the scene, was to find fun inadvertently, just when we adults were thinking life grim. On one occasion, when as yet I knew scarcely anyone in Washington, I was standing all alone in my strange kitchen wondering whether my day was ever going to consist of more than a pile of washing-up and gobbledygook from this robust, all-demanding toddler. The washer on the tap was worn and a relentless drip pinged coldly and rhythmically into the already tepid washing-up water. I had no idea where to find a plumber nor even whether that was the word one used in the States. I dared not telephone Hugh's school and ask for help on such a small matter. There was no one else to talk to. Our pre-Revolution clapboard cottage was set in parkland; we had no near neighbours, as yet no one to invite in for a cup of coffee; the future held no further prospect than the need for me to clear up kitchens. I felt utterly alone and helpless.

Suddenly there were insistent cries from Penelope:

"'Ook, Mummy. Mummy, 'ook!"

I looked, expecting to have to scrape from the floor yet another soggy rusk, dropped accidentally-on-purpose.

But no. Her merry eyes were chasing something on the ceiling.

"'Ook, Mummy . . . See de firefly?"

And there on the ceiling flickered and danced an elfin light.

It was some time before I realised how the sun had broken through a cloudy day and transformed the drear of the dripping tap's ripple into a sun-dance on the ceiling.

Penelope grew; the Poor People marched on Washington; Martin Luther King and Robert Kennedy were shot; the blacks rioted; we were under curfew and, quite unexpectedly, bouncy, friend-of-all Penelope stopped the traffic in Washington.

She had not woken up in her usual way, one morning. The sub-tropical heat was stifling and so I sat my strangely floppy little girl on my lap and offered her a cup of rose-hip water. Instead of accepting it she started to jerk her right arm spasmodically, but continued to flop against me in a dozy way. After about half an hour of this we telephoned the doctor's office and asked advice.

"It's probably a heat convulsion, common in young children in this heat. Call me back, Mrs Allan, if it goes on for more than three minutes... Half an hour already? I'll be right round."

So she was whirled, to the accompaniment of a siren on the doctor's own car, to D.C. Children's Hospital, quite unconscious in a prolonged series of convulsions. She recovered within twenty-four hours.

They told us she must be hypersensitive to the tension in Washington, because she was so intelligent and naturally responsive. They told us not to worry.

Washington went on seething politically; the cicadas' incessant sizzling jarred on our nerves through the torpor of humid nights; the wealthy made for the mountains and New England, while we checked our papers preparatory to our return to Old England, our short-term engagement in the States having expired.

I was heavily seasick on board the Queen Elizabeth and Penelope knew why. She loved patting my front gently and telling strangers that that was the baby in her mother's tummy.

Then there was a series of firsts: her first awareness of England, of relations, especially grandparents, of the shyness of English children, of the smells and pinkness of Lincolnshire pigs and, then, of November 5th fireworks and their particular way of expressing Penelope's wonder and joy at all creation.

That night she had another series of convulsions. There followed precisely the same routine of hospitalisation, recovery and the injunction not to worry.

December came. The checkout girl at the local super-market was one of the many who were dragged out to a waiting pram to admire "my sister Chooliet". Juliet was, we hoped, to be the friend Penelope had been looking for since her return to England ... but not quite yet. "Chooliet" couldn't even put her own thumb in her mouth without the tender guidance of big sister. In the meantime friends at playschool might fill the gap.

One Monday in January, Penelope's great moment, her enrolment at playschool arrived. So did a big "head hurts". It was in fact so violent that she agreed to go and lie on the settee for a few minutes. Every so often she assured me that she was "nearly all better", at least enough to go and find her new friends at playschool. But the hours passed and in fact her ache grew so bad that by evening she was only too glad to go with her father to let the doctor make her "head hurt" all better.

He found nothing wrong. A stranger to Penelope's ways, he suggested that she might be jealous of her baby sister.

That night her pain was so violent that she screamed as if with meningitis. A much more sober little girl donned her January overcoat next morning, this time sure that the doctor would recognise that there was something wrong and "mend the big head hurts" at last.

He found nothing.

Tuesday afternoon passed in alternating periods of screams of pain and resigned silence. By late evening we were suspicious of the deep sleep that seemed to have come upon her. This time we called the doctor to us – the head of the practice. He brusquely declared that Penelope was in a coma.

Within hours she was again stopping the traffic, this time en route to Great Ormond Street Hospital for Sick Children,

London. Late that night a brain tumour occupying half her brain was diagnosed.

On the Wednesday morning I stood beside her bed, trying to call her back to consciousness as she lay dying.

"Penelope! Pelpy, darling. It's Mummy." Her hand moved, but it was bandaged and I dared not hurt it by taking it. (I learned afterwards that I could have done. The bandages were merely to prevent her from pulling the tubes from the other parts of her body.)

"Please, Lord, help her. Pelpy! Penelope!"

Then a strange surprise. I had been used in prayer to a monologue with my God, during which I tried to imagine how he would view the situation. Now, for the first time, entirely new thoughts shot into my mind, presenting the matter to me from a fresh standpoint. I found he was really talking to me:

"Why are you calling her back?"

"Because I want you to heal her, please. Oh, please. PLEASE."

"In your English lessons you're always quoting Browning: 'Man's reach should exceed his grasp, or what's a heaven for?' What *is* heaven, in your understanding?"

"Oh, a place of bliss I suppose."

"Bliss. Meaning what?"

"Utter joy, fulfilment, reassurance."

"Why, then, are you depriving her of that?"

"Because I love her. After all, I'm her mother. You don't know what that's like. I've looked after her all her life, shielded her from measles, traffic, any hint of unhappiness. There was all that pain at her birth. She's mine and I want her. *Please* will you heal her. I know you can. So please do so. I do believe. PLEASE!"

"One moment. *Who* looked after her all her life? Didn't I look after you both, especially at her birth? Who made you her mother?"

"You did. But you don't know what this is like to me. Look at her, lying there swathed in bandages and stuck with tubes. I can't even cuddle her or take her hand."

"Who gave you this love, this mother's love. Did I not create all the mothers that have ever lived? Does my love not surpass all the love I've ever instilled into all those droplets of my vast creation? My love is utterly boundless and you're holding your daughter back from receiving it with me now."

"Well, if you want her now, you must have her. She's yours, after all."

Three minutes after that Penelope stopped breathing. I was fully aware that the real Penelope was still in the room, above me, somewhere in the region of the ceiling, but definitely going away, as cheerfully as ever...

Soon after her death I had a picture of Penelope peeping in at me from a brilliantly sunny world. She was swinging on the hand of a tall, athletic man. She showed him her mummy and daddy.

"Look after them, won't you." And she was off, her hand in his, full of trust, fun and the spirit of exploration, *her* side of death.

*   *   *

Now another entry in the London *Times*, incredibly in the Deaths column, and also in the *Washington Post*:

> On January 22nd 1969 at Great Ormond Street Hospital, London, England. Penelope Jane Allan died aged 2½ formerly of Washington, D.C., daughter of Hugh and Rosalind, sister of Juliet. Services and interment were held in England.

There was to be no shaking off those facts.

We had driven through the January traffic in the drizzle to the Registrar's office. I'd visited Penelope's bandaged and sheeted body in the mortuary and kissed an ice-cold farewell, but of course she herself was not there. Carved over the tiny altar in Great Ormond Street mortuary chapel are a pair of child's hands reaching up towards and being enclosed by a strong man's hands. Underneath is the inscription:

Is it well with the child?
Yes, it is very well.

That, too, we knew as a fact.

Penelope's life was brief, but in the combination of her life and death lay the seeds of a new life, a complete transformation, for me, whether I wanted it or not. I was to discover a new dimension in my relationships to both God and other people. Above all, this was to be the beginning of new adventures in faith.

2. The Broken-hearted

Only three days had passed since Penelope's first "head-hurts", and it was still January; a long time till the spring. Juliet was still uncommunicatively content, to the point where I wondered whether she was perhaps retarded. But life was bustling along apace in the ordinary world of Slough.

As soon as we arrived home I began to catch glimpses of a power at work, almost imperceptibly, in the activities of people around me. There were little hints of care and love.

The first was a bright flash. As we carried Juliet in her carry-cot up our narrow path in the sleet and gloom of winter I saw on the back doorstep, not the expected accumulation of three deliveries of milk, but the day's supply neatly arranged, and there triumphant, a pure white vase with twelve red roses. The accompanying card showed that they had been ordered from Washington, D.C., in thankfulness and love for Penelope. We were sad that so few people in England knew her well enough to talk of her with us.

But the Lord knew better than to leave us thus alone. In what seemed no time at all "Auntie Bender", Penelope's godmother and my college friend, had arrived to hear all about the little girl who had spent only one afternoon in the garden with her. Standing about five times as tall as Penelope, gentle and perceptive Brenda had blown myriad bubbles across the lawn and with Penelope had chased their rainbows a few inches above the grass. They had hoped one day to discuss other matters together, but they had shared the exhilaration and wonder of creation already. Brenda was a sounding-board for memories.

Then there were the children from all around. They had stood a little apart from Penelope when she first arrived from the States because she talked of cookies and jello. It hurt for a time to walk past children at play. Every so often one would have the same black curls or chunky shape and my subconscious would be full of sudden hope. Quite suddenly they were all coming to our door: big, tough-looking girls of eight or nine and toddler boys, asking to play in our house, giving me their grubby pictures done in a playschool Penelope had never attended, shyly hoping they were acceptable.

On the other hand a depressing experience which all who are bereaved go through is to find that friends and neighbours, not knowing how lonely we feel about our loss, actually avoid contact and go to the length of crossing the street or turning in the opposite direction in order to evade what might be an embarrassing or distressing encounter.

The funeral itself still had to be arranged. Hugh and I agreed that cremation was the simplest way of disposing of what were, after all, only remains. But we did want to proclaim our conviction that this was Penelope's first birthday in Heaven and so a time for great rejoicing. It is very difficult to express that conviction at a time when the world expects us to express only our deprivation and grief. However, the funeral service does it all for us. All we had to do was invite our friends home for a fourpenny ice-cream, Penelope's favourite treat, in order to celebrate with her and to give thanks that her life had been so full, glad and free of disillusion and despair.

Again there were indications of this strange power at work. Not only did we receive daily telephone calls from grandparents, but also many letters, some of which challenged me because they denied that God's will is ever achieved through death. One, from a clergyman, declared that God is unable to do anything to counter the power of evil, but merely allows it all to happen. One of the most incisive came from America, to the effect that the loss of a beloved child clears the way for a closer love of God. I had to reply to all these letters, to deny the things I knew from my new experience to be untrue and defeatist, and to acknowledge and be thankful for the things which helped me gradually to understand.

At another level altogether, the neighbours turned up on the day of the funeral with buns for the guests who coped with their fourpenny ice-creams according to their kind – grieving or celebrating. An uncle elbowed his robust and rosy way in among the gloomier, proclaiming, "I've brought you a big tray of onions – to help you cry, because you really should!" Little did anyone then know how at night I wept silently into the pillow because of my deprivation; but there he was making me laugh with onions!

I began to realise that all these little glimpses of love and compassion, expressed by shy children, bewildered neighbours, appalled relations, philosophers and garden enthusiasts, were glimpses of parts of the Body of Christ at work, cherishing me – the toes, the hands, the arms, the legs of his Body, all doing their part. The Resurrection was a reality. Jesus was with me, concerned, gently soothing each dragging hurt.

The tables were soon to be turned, beginning the very next day. I now had to pass on these signs of love which I had received, to those who, as I had been, were beset by fear, despair, or even the desire for revenge. The first to arrive in the last category was the Press. Reporters came, wanting us to sue the medical profession for negligence. We told them to go away, because any more death, destruction, and all malice and revenge were out of the question. We had seen our relations reconciled in their little differences through this event. Where now was a way through to reconciliation and forgiveness with the medical profession? Almost the next day our family doctor arrived, tweaking his trousers in alarm as he sat expressing his apology for failure to detect such a serious illness. I was mortified and filled with a strange new compassion for the man in his fear.

A postcard arrived from the Health Department, announcing its concern for me in "my bereavement" (filled in personally) and offering an appointment with the psychiatric social worker on (filled in) at (filled in). I telephoned to explain that I had already received and was receiving an abundance of help, but would be glad to share my new understanding and acceptance with anyone in a similar position.

The psychiatric social worker suggested that I call on a Jamaican family who lived just round the corner. I had never seen a coloured person in the vicinity, let alone a family, and so it was with some puzzlement that I wheeled Juliet's pram round to visit at the address given. The curtains were drawn, the venetian blinds blanked off; I decided that the household were either away or still in bed, mid-morning. Nevertheless, I rang the bell briefly and waited. Very soon there were noises within. A plump Jamaican lady with a rasping voice enquired what I wanted. I explained as best I knew how, and was invited to return the following week. The next time I called I was invited in. Juliet. co-operatively fast asleep, stayed outside, under the window in her pram. I soon realised that Juliet's somnolence was a blessing. My new friend had had but one child and now was completely alone, until her husband came in from work at the end of the day. As I sat in the still-shrouded living room, she told me how she had been ill in bed. Her four-year-old daughter had been trying to be Mummy in the kitchen. She had climbed onto a chair and reached over the gas-cooker in order to fetch down a cup and saucer. She had not noticed that the gas-jets were lit, cooking lunch. In no time at all she was alight, her pretty little West Indian petticoats engulfed in flames. The mother had weathered the funeral and the family gathering and the fuss, but now all that was over and she had no one to care for, no one who really needed her, nothing to live for. All her love and careful cherishing of the child had resulted in nothing. Here were the little clothes and toys. But where was her darling?

Suddenly I realised that she had come to the end of her story and that I was supposed to be helpful. All I could do was to tell her how I had had a similar experience. This seemed to be an encouragement for more confidences and here I was completely out of my depth. She had a deep sense that, had she not succumbed to illness, had she supervised her daughter's helpfulness more carefully, had she taught her daughter earlier the danger of gas-jets on a cooker, the little girl would still be bouncing around, cheering her mother up in this alien all-white environment. I, too, had questioned the might-have-beens in Penelope's life. But her cancer was inexplicable and nothing to do with my treatment of her. Now how could I relieve this woman of this great weight? I was nonplussed.

A few weeks later my new friend called at our house, but refused to cross the threshold. She had come, she explained, to tell me that she intended to make a visit the following week. Dressed very elegantly and wearing a hat, she arrived on the appointed day. We exchanged formalities and coffee. I noticed how flared her nostrils were and how fiercely her eyes flashed as she recalled the events of her daughter's life. She had now been trying to get in touch with the world of the dead and had consulted a Voodoo priest, but to little avail. She wondered whether perhaps I could reach the realm of the dead, and placate the spirits she had offended. I began to realise how arrogant I had been in my claim to the Health Authorities that I had something to share with anyone. In fact I felt utterly apart from this poor lady. She was suffering in ways I could not understand.

Meanwhile at home I was receiving virtually daily visits from Grace, a stout-bottomed health visitor. She was officially making the statutory visits to our now not-so-newborn Juliet but she was also making these an occasion for pouring out her own troubles. Grace, a single lady, was holding down her job with great difficulty and in real physical pain. She had hurt her back while lifting an elderly patient and lived in constant dread of being allocated another lifting job. If she were discovered to be unfit, possibly permanently disabled, then her job was gone. I suggested she consulted a doctor not connected with her practice. But there were complications of medical etiquette, hard to circumvent. All I could do was sit and listen.

However, something in me connected with Penelope's own concern for people's hurt was making me really troubled on Grace's account. I did have the beginnings of a new kind of compassion; but again I was unable to provide a solution to the problem.

We now needed to produce another companion for Juliet who was beginning to sit up and take a lot of friendly notice of everything and everyone. The dentist had told me that I should have impacted wisdom teeth removed, and that I should not be pregnant at the time. So we agreed that I should go into hospital during the half-term holiday, just as soon as Hugh was available to look after Juliet. I was admitted one day before my operation into a hospital that specialised in both dentistry and the healing of severe burns. Adjacent to my ward was the Children's Burns Unit.

Perfectly fit, I had a day to waste in hospital, interspersed with the usual pre-operative blood and lung tests. I could hear the children next door, some running around and laughing, many moaning and sobbing. An orderly explained that they were all very bored because the teacher who usually came to entertain and occupy them was away, it being half-term holiday. Tentatively, but with a great desire to reach out to the children and love them, I admitted that I was a qualified teacher and was willing to go and tell them a home-made story or invent a game.

Before I knew what was happening I was following a nurse into the Burns Ward. "Quiet, children, please. Here's teacher!" I was horrified. The children were of all ages from five to sixteen, variously incapacitated; I had absolutely no idea what lessons in hospital for such a motley crew could possibly mean. My escort half marched out as swiftly as she had swept in, and I was alone. A child took my hand and led me to the teacher's cupboard. It was locked.

"But there are some toys under these benches. Look, you just lift the seats up."

"Stupid. They're all broken!" sneered an older boy. "You can't do anything with them."

I lifted the bench lids and tried to sort out a collection of bricks and a few pieces of Lego. There was a doll with only one leg.

A noise like a flute crept into my ear from above me, but the flute was breathy and became intelligible as a voice. A shrivelled hand, with distorted stubs for fingers, reached down to mine and the voice breathed,

"There is another leg. It's hers. It's over here."

I looked up, to see who was trying to communicate. Two eyes, two nostril holes, no nose, a contorted, shrivelled escape-hatch of a mouth, no hair; a young girl was trying to help me. She and I soon became good friends. While we talked and invented games for the others I inspected her wounds, realising that her face was gradually being rebuilt from patches of skin grafted from the rest of her body. She showed me what operations had so far been performed on her, and I was amazed at her delight and open friendliness.

When I left the Burns Unit I asked after her parents, wondering how to help them in what must be deep misery. I remembered my Jamaican friend.

"Jenny's parents? She has no parents. Well, that's to say, they don't want to see her ever again."

Everything in me cried out to ask permission to foster Jenny. But I knew any enquiry about my recent history would show that I was in no condition to make such a decision. When I mentioned the matter to Hugh he too thought this was not the right moment to take on such a responsibility.

So again I wanted to help, to share the love I was receiving, but was powerless.

Staying in Slough became a more and more dreary prospect. Soon after Penelope's death we started looking around for somewhere else for Hugh to teach and for us all to live. I was now pregnant again, but in no way was the new life within going to be a substitute for what I had lost. Whatever was growing inside me had a particularly vigorous personality all its own!

Hugh was appointed Head of English at Stamford School, Lincolnshire. Stamford is a mellow market town set alongside the River Welland, its grey Collyweston slate skyline punctuated by ancient spires and towers. The house we found for our tiny family was disproportionately large. We had just our one baby, Juliet, and the Bulge. The tall Victoria semi had nine bedrooms. The top floor, let off as a flat, would pay the mortgage; the potentialities of the remaining three floors stretched the mind; the view out across open countryside was peaceful, and the cost of the whole no more than that of a three-bedroomed estate house. Something in me was confirming that here was great hope and adventure in the future if we took this on. As we left after the viewing we noticed that the Latin inscription on the coat of arms in the stained glass front door read: *Deo adiuvante vincam* – With God's help I shall triumph.

However was God going to help me triumph? Over what? I was to find the answer only over the years. Carved in the grey stone arch above the door was an owl surmounting a rose – wisdom and love combined.

My Bulge emerged easily and vigorously as Rupert, a dark-haired, good-humoured bundle of male self-assertion.

The social life of a school community, with coffee mornings for the young mums, was occupying some of my time, interspersed with a bit of part-time teaching of my own. In the midst of this someone came to share her great loss of a mongol daughter. Mrs Turner and her husband had fostered a happy, outgoing little girl who was severely handicapped, but full of joy. She had developed an infection which was not detected soon enough by her doctor, and she had died. Now, years later, Mrs Turner was full of bitterness and a desire to wreak vengeance on the medical profession. I was, as usual, able to pin on my accolade of shared experience, but again was quite unable really to help; not so much a case of the blind leading the blind, as the helpless helping the helpless. I lent her my collection of sympathy letters in the hope that she might be able to salvage some wisdom from them, as indeed I had. But they referred to my situation, rather than hers.

There was a phone-call, urgent and perplexed, from a

doctor friend. She was upset and anxious to know precisely how a newly bereaved mother might feel. Her own close friend Anna had gone on a family holiday with her brother and his wife. During preparations for an outing Anna's toddler daughter had wandered off into the garden. She did not return. After a long search, she was found, face down, in the swimming pool. The family outing was forgotten and the much-cherished little girl whirled off, like Penelope, in an ambulance to the nearest hospital. Everything was done to try to revive her, but in fact the situation in the garden had been hopeless. The family returned from their holiday, stunned by an unforeseeable and horribly premature bereavement.

It was difficult to express all that a mother might be feeling at such a time, especially as I did not know the family concerned. But at that time I was convinced that a way of honouring Penelope's existence was to use my experience to reach out to others in the same plight. So I got in touch with Anna. She talked; we talked; I talked; on and on. We became loving friends, but I felt all along that there was no way in which I could bring real healing to her or her husband. I could only encourage her to face the whole experience and to try to accept it.

A new awareness of people's distress and their desperate, if often smothered, shouts for help, was being forced upon me. Again and again I was being brought up against divorced people, the newly bereaved and the very ill. I was invited to rejoin the Samaritans, with whom I had already worked in Bedford, and to do Marriage Guidance Counselling, but I was unable to cope even with the needs of the people around me. The world about me was sick. I longed, for the sake of the new life Penelope was enjoying, to bring help. But I found that even the sophisticated counselling techniques which I had been taught left me feeling frustrated and inadequate in the face of real hurt. I was learning that I, of myself, had nothing with which to bind up the broken hearts that surrounded me. Wisdom and Love were the insignia carved over our front door, but for them to cease to be stony symbols and take flesh in my life, I definitely needed something more.

3. Something More

> I will give you a new heart and a new mind. I will
> take away your stubborn heart of stone and give
> you an obedient heart. I will put my spirit in you ...
> (Ezek. 36:26,27)

Hanna was the German wife of a garage owner. During my
first few years in Stamford I encountered her only in the
context of having my car serviced or refuelled. Blonde and
attractive, she was always friendly.

I had spent a very busy winter buzzing from my part-time
job as a lecturer at the College of Further Education to the
playschool, and home to get the family meals, now for three
young children, Bridget, the fourth and by far the hungriest,
having arrived. One Spring day I whirled in, en route to the
College, to buy some petrol and conversationally asked after
Hanna.

"They can't do anything more for her," answered her
husband.

"Whatever is the matter?"

"Didn't you know? She's been having the heaviest possible
traction all winter. Two slipped discs, a trapped sciatic
nerve; they can do nothing."

I felt ashamed that I had been so heedless of my
neighbour. My children and music had taken up much of my
time and interest when I was not teaching. I had not noticed
Hanna's absence. Now I was being told which convalescent
hospital she was in and the visiting hours.

Visiting the "backs" ward was a curious experience. At my
entry each prostrate figure flipped an eager head to see who

had come and relaxed it in disappointment – except Hanna, who welcomed me gladly. I exchanged the usual pleasantries about the ward and the treatment she had received, and, maintaining my helpful smile, registered her total lack of hope for the future. I gave Hanna the conventional bunch of flowers and left in embarrassment.

As I drove away I said a routine prayer for the sick, especially Hanna. Then I felt a sudden burst of indignation that she should be in this condition and I so incapable of giving any real help. As I drove along I expostulated to God, indignant that he should allow anyone so lithe and in the prime of life to continue to be so incapacitated. I also made it very clear that I objected to being so useless in this time of need.

Into my head immediately slid a reminder of a telephone conversation I had had with a local curate recently, Tim Dicken:

"What have you been so busy doing lately, Ros? You haven't been to the Power, Praise and Healing Services. There was one last night. I went along to see what happened."

"Who was doing what?"

"Trevor Dearing was preaching. He has the gift of healing."

"Is he a quack?"

"People were falling down as he prayed for them."

"Oh dear. That's no good if you're an old dear with arthritis or a game leg, is it? *Must* be a quack."

"Trevor's a reverend gentleman, Ros. And do you honestly think the Creator Holy Spirit's going to cause anyone to be injured while his power is upon them for healing?"

"Do you think he's O.K., then?"

"All I can say is, go along and see."

I was frustrated by Tim's refusal to commit himself and thus influence me – frustrated and tantalised.

I returned to the convalescent hospital the next week. Hanna was not present. She was in Peterborough having an X-ray check-up to establish that the situation had not changed. With some relief that I did not have to encounter her on a religious matter face-to-face, I scribbled a hasty note on one of her paper tissues explaining that I was not in any way connected with what might be a quack ministry, but was willing to go along with her when she was discharged, to a Power, Praise and Healing Meeting.

Some weeks later I met Hanna at the garage:

"So you're home? And better?"

"No, not better. I can only stand stiff and straight like this or lie down. Otherwise I am in tremendous pain. But it is good to be home and I am certainly willing to come to Trevor Dearing. I do attend the village church at Tinwell, you know."

The visit to a Power, Praise and Healing meeting was soon arranged and we went along to see what it was all about. When we arrived, the singing had already begun, and I was immediately put off; the choruses and the hand-clapping, the arm-waving that was going on offended my cultural sensibilities. As fresh people arrived, they seemed to be greeting one another with real love and joy. Reared in the stiff-upper-lip restraint of the Anglican tradition, I found all this disconcerting and alien.

Settled in the position of an outside observer in the back row of the gallery, I began to examine the proceedings more carefully – and once again I found my God taking up my arguments one by one.

"All this clapping and arm-raising..."

"Look at the words they are singing."

"O clap your hands all you people."

"Lift up holy hands and bless the Lord."

So I could not really fault that.

"But, Lord, they're repeating these unmusical tunes again and again, until they become meaningless."

"You do the same in your worship: *'Kyrie eleison,* Lord have mercy, Christ have mercy.' You are a hypocrite. You pride yourself on your intellect and your carefully thought-out faith. Paul was the same. But when he came to know me personally he went to stay with Simon Peter. He was no scholar, had a strong Galilean accent and probably still smelt of fish. But Peter had spent three years with me, and so Paul could learn from someone who knew me as a real friend and brother. These people know me like that, too. I wish you did."

Trevor Dearing was now praying with gifts of knowledge for some of the sick who were present. I myself had had a heavy day showing Rupert the sights of London, and was trying to hide another of my recurrent attacks of sinusitis. My nose was dripping freely and I was dabbing at it with a handkerchief. I scowled round critically and watched for signs of instantaneous healing. We asked the Lord to heal paralysis, tumours, epilepsy and "someone present with painful sinuses." I peered down on the heads of the congregation below.

"Amen!" At last we could get on with the meeting. No one seemed to be leaping around with delight at their healing. More choruses.

"Feeling better?" Hanna smiled.

"Better? From what?" I muttered.

"Your nose seems clearer."

I breathed deeply. So it was. I was astonished. No one could have been further removed from praying the prayer of faith. Yet here I was, healed of my sinusitis.

The sermon was witty and totally absorbing. Only afterwards did I realise it had lasted well over half an hour, and I was used to ten minutes at the most. Then those in need of prayer were invited to come forward for the laying on of hands. This was where Hanna came in, if she would.

"Go on, be a devil," I suggested. "Sorry – wrong expression. Are you going to try it? I'll come with you."

Hanna and I crept down the gallery stairs and joined the queue of those going forward. As we neared the front I felt terribly conspicuous and out of place and, coward that I was, slid into the nearest empty pew.

I watched, fascinated, as Hanna stood, rigidly upright in her pain. She did not fall as hands were laid on her.

I rejoined her as she returned, smiling peacefully,

"How was it?" I asked.

"I hate to disappoint you," Hanna replied, "but I have not got an ache or pain anywhere in my body."

Hanna's healing was complete. The next morning and thereafter she was able to lift heavy objects, to move around freely, to bend and stretch, to give glory to her Lord.

We attended several such monthly meetings with a growing confidence that what the various speakers were saying and doing was evidence of a tremendous power, present and available for all who would receive it.

One Saturday morning I was wondering about all this as I wandered into Woolworth's, pushing the pram with its double load of young children. Standing talking to someone else was Anne Dearing, Trevor's wife.

"Talk to her and ask her about this 'something more'," nudged the voice.

"On a Saturday morning, among all these shoppers? No."

"I said, 'Talk to her'."

"Well, only if she is still standing there when we have made the full circuit of the sweet counter."

Of course, she was; and I did.

Ann has told me since how she had indeed seen me in the gallery the night before. She had wanted to help me then. Now all the advice she would give after these tremendous displays of God's power at work in people's lives was:

"Go home and gather round you a little group of friends who will pray and read the Bible with you."

It seemed too trite, too straightforward and, among the friends I had, far too difficult.

However, after many false moves, I did manage to discuss such things with several friends. A few of them, those who did not feel that the Bible had been studied in school and was dull and finished with, started to meet regularly to read and to pray. Among them was Hazel who, like me, had read Catherine Marshall's *Something More*. We were eager to find out much more about what the Lord was doing in these big, interdenominational, Holy-Spirit-filled rallies.

We tried to discuss these matters in our group, but interest was minimal. One lady was rather embarrassed at the thought that she might have to take part in "excesses", such as speaking in tongues, or having to hug someone. Two of the men in the group relished disputes on interpretation of the original Greek, or even the Hebrew of the more obscure books of the Old Testament. One was convinced that he had been a Christian since birth and so being born again was unnecessary for him. One had a great desire to know the "something more" we talked of, but he was an officer in the R.A.F. and did not want to step out of line. But one way and another, Hazel and I were discerning between different approaches to Christianity and becoming more and more definite about what we wanted.

Some time later, at another rally, there was a sermon about the Holy Spirit. I had known, ever since confirmation, the logical theory about the Holy Spirit. "It" was the third person of the Trinity; "it" was not Father, was not Son, but was God. In my picture it was the base line of a triangle, the glue that joined the two realities, a mystery, an "it". Nevertheless I had already witnessed the fact that "it" was around and active nowadays, and the gifts Paul writes of in I Corinthians 12 were abundantly evident at the Power, Praise and Healing meetings.

Now it was also being pointed out to me that I could see the fruits of the Spirit around me: there was the obvious love amongst the people in the congregation and the joy in their worship; many of the testimonies I heard talked of experiences weathered with patience and genuine, almost amused, humility. There was no forcing into any pattern of conformity; all was gentleness.

If we now felt that perhaps we had not yet received the fullness of the Holy Spirit, the preacher was continuing, if perhaps what we knew of the Spirit was somewhat impersonal (I remembered my concept of an "it"); if we yearned for the power of the Holy Spirit so to fill us to the brim that it spilled over to help heal others and bring great joy to all around us, then we could now come forward and ask for something more.

I looked around the church, at the wooden but sheltering gallery over my head, and wondered whether I cared any longer what people might think if I emerged from my side pew and crept forward as unobtrusively as possible. I saw others, all sorts and shapes of men and women jostling each other eagerly towards the front; saw my friend Hazel calm and dignified, making her way among them ... and suddenly I was there, too. We found a place to kneel amidst the mêlée of expectant people, some standing, many with heads bowed and arms upraised. We repeated a very simple prayer of repentance and of openness to receive the fullness of the blessed Holy Spirit of Jesus. We were assured that once we had invited him into our hearts and lives there would be no going back on the part of God. He was with us always, right to the end of time itself. We received the baptism of the Holy Spirit.

Some who were there were so overwhelmed immediately by the power that they were receiving that they swooned, seraphic smiles on their faces. Others joined in the choruses now being sung with jubilation and radiant thankfulness. One man with a little goatee beard actually started to bounce from one foot to the other in a very jolly way down the aisle to the very back of the church and thence to his pew. Those near chuckled and clapped the rhythm, in order to encourage him. All was freedom.

Inside, deep down I was aware that I knew for the first time the person who is the Holy Spirit. My Creator had, before, been a person whose majesty and authority in ordering his creation were awesome; my Saviour Jesus had been incarnate and knew what it was like to be me; now the Holy Spirit was showing me the joyous life and the exhilaration that lie in the heart of the Godhead. Someone earlier mentioned the Creator Holy Spirit's cherishing. Now that was to become a reality too.

4. Foolish Things

FOR SALE: ex-library van. Fifteen years old. Suitable chippy or pop-group. £390.

So read the torn advertisement. Found by someone's grandfather in Skegness, torn from a Louth newspaper, it now lay ready to be screwed up in my hands in Stamford. But there was something fascinating about the wording.

Christian books had begun to form a new attraction for me. When I was growing up I thought of such publications as dull crimson volumes; old sermons, biographies of missionaries long since dead, recipes for self-improvement mostly leading only to self-satisfaction, impressive, academic, semi-encyclopaedias, a half dozen of which stood untouched on the school library shelves. Now I had, with my friend Hazel, discovered an abundance of really exciting, colourful, contemporary paperbacks, which we had been buying gleefully for our church bookstalls – books which spoke about the new life in the Holy Spirit which we had just discovered.

Two or three years earlier I had worked my way through *The True Wilderness* by H. A. Williams and Vanstone's *Love's Endeavour, Love's Expense*. The earnest search of these two writers after a deeper knowledge of God had encouraged me. Then John Taylor's *The Go-Between God* had led me much further on in my understanding of the Holy Spirit's work of giving glory to the other two members of the Trinity. But it was only in the past few months that I had become absorbed in the adventures and experiences of people whose lives had been turned upside down in their personal encounter with the Holy Spirit of Jesus: Corrie Ten Boom in *The Hiding Place*, Catherine Marshall in *Something More*, Brother Andrew in *God's Smuggler*, Fred Lemon in *Breakout* and Doreen Irvine in *From Witchcraft to Christ*. Such stories were so exciting that I no longer needed to lace my "serious" reading with lighter, secular stuff; with their pace, humour and challenge they fed my spirit as never before. It was not long before Hazel and I were reading, parallel to these autobiographies, the same writers' recipes for the way we too could live according to God's leading.

Hazel and I now wanted the whole town to catch on to what we had found. During a week of celebration officially for the Queen's Silver Jubilee, unofficially of our own glorious new discoveries, we held a mammoth book fair. We hired the local Roman Catholic Hall, it being the only one not in use for playschool, or other such activities. All the families involved sent their children out with invitations to people in their areas to give second-hand books of any kind for Christian Aid. After a week, our excited children were sent out with barrows, boxes and baskets, to collect what had been given.

Juliet now aged eight, armed herself with a small rucksack; Rupert, a sturdy seven, followed suit; together they visited houses all around the block where our house stood, watching out eagerly for their own favourites – books about making things, adventure stories, or books about cars and farm machinery. Bridget, still only four years old, "helped" cheerily to sort the books her way.

Many thousands of books were accumulated in some stables. Hugh and I spent evenings and weekends with our friends, sorting the splendid from the sordid, stacking books into pile upon pile, and pricing with as much discrimination as we could muster. We grew dustier and drearier as we worked far into the night, often not noticing the first editions and the fine prints lurking among the cobwebs.

By Jubilee Week, 1977, a whole gang of workers, Roman Catholic, Anglican, Methodist, Free Church, Pentecostal,

Salvation Army, Baptist had crammed that hall with second-hand books all round the walls. Spread down the centre were all the new Christian books which we could acquire, with next to no funds, but plenty of goodwill from the publishers.

We noticed that people queued each day before opening time – queued with sacks! This was when we realised that the specialist and antiquarian book ring was in operation. It was a tussle to know whether to try to beat them at their own game or whether with openness and trust to ask those who knew the market value of books to give to Christian Aid what was appropriate. Mostly we decided on the latter course. It was thrilling to be shown, confidentially, that a book we were selling quite ordinarily was a very rare specimen, and that the purchaser wanted to give many pounds more than we had asked. Of course there must have been those which disappeared into the hands of the hard-bitten and acquisitive, but we were beginning to realise that love must abound, even in business!

To that end, a coffee-counter was set up in the far corner of the hall, and those who wanted to rest, to browse in their purchases, or to share their problems and joys, settled there. Children had invariably found bargains which they showed each other over cold drinks. Grandmothers rested weary feet while their menfolk were absorbed in stories from their youth, now long since out of print; students and the antiquarian vultures, well satisfied, were having their hearts warmed – all the family congregated under one roof. One person remarked,

"I can't keep away from this place. I wish I'd brought my bed."

A book party was arranged for the end of the week. Those who had enjoyed a new Christian book were asked to speak about it, so as to recommend it to others. Curiously, the whole event grew into a big discussion about the need for a Christian bookshop in the town.

I myself had had a curious "waking dream" that had pursued me so clearly and persistently that I'd had to tell the others about it. I did so, at first tentatively and incredulously, then with increasing confidence as I realised the potential of what had come into my head that night.

A middle-aged, pear-shaped lady was plodding up a narrow street with a laden shopping trolley. On her right was an old book shop, the dull windows revealing leather-bound volumes and antiquarian prints. But in the foreground was a scatter of her favourite Mills & Boon romances at only five pence per copy! Here was a way to escape the drag of all her family.

She heaved her trolley into the shop entrance and forged ahead to find her favourites. This involved negotiating a colourful display of new paperbacks. Flat on its back, directly under her nose, was something about the Christian and drug abuse. Maybe her Tommy was into drugs? She thumbed her way through to the "symptoms" section. Dilated pupils? Listlessness? Yes, those were certainly familiar. But whatever could she do about any of it? Back to Mills & Boon.

At this point into the dream came someone whom I knew. Jenny, mother of four teenagers, beamed round the stack of books.

"Can I help?"

"I'm wondering what to do. This book's told me a lot, but I need more."

"Come on through here to the coffee bar. There's a hot cuppa in there – and it's free. If it's drugs you're worried about, I know a very warm-hearted Christian doctor who helps at the Peterborough drug centre..."

There, in the cosy depths of the shop was far more than a cheap escape: human care and a stepping-stone towards help.

There the dream ended.

There were those who pointed out that the local bookshop already had a small section of religious books and Bibles, presumably all that a small market town could stomach. But there were others who were adamant that in the books that

had been sold during the week there was a new dimension –
in fact New Life itself.

There was talk of premises and property, of places that
could be turned into shops, of opposition from planning
committees. Gradually we came down to earth and admitted
that the sum of all the gifts we could pool amounted to barely
enough to rent a barn – and one of those was certainly not
available within the shopping precinct of Stamford.

We each agreed to pray, keep our ears and eyes open for
possible premises and share our discoveries at a meeting
three months thence.

Now, several weeks later, I was standing in the middle of
the kitchen and thinking about this absurd advertisement. A
van? "Suitable for chippy or pop group"?

Only the evening before we had heard an address on the
text:

"God hath chosen the foolish things of the world to
confound the wise; and God hath chosen the weak things of
the world to confound the things which are mighty." (1 Cor.
1:27, A.V.)

Abraham set out from Ur with all his wives, concubines
and cattle but he did not know where he was going. Noah
built an ark when it was not even raining. Paul risked his life
again and again for the sake of a Christ he had met only in a
vision.

Here we were, a very small group of friends of assorted
ages and interests, with no funds except our ordinary
earnings, and no experience whatsoever of running such a
venture. Perhaps we were not being entirely realistic. The
idea of this vehicle had been discounted by most of the
others; none of us was convinced that our vocation lay in
maintaining a dilapidated, if not rust-riddled, library van.
And whoever among us could decide whether the fifteen-
year-old vehicle advertised was in sound condition? Those
who knew about car maintenance were not prepared to take
on anything more than three years old. Hugh, despite his
love of mementoes of by-gone days, declined to take on this

responsibility while committed to a full-time teaching job; the keenest interest was shown by a young lorry-driver who wanted to buy the engine only, because of its antique value!

All these cogitations were taking place amongst the washing-up on a Saturday morning. The foolishness of buying a fifteen-year-old van... Wherever would we keep it?... Nevertheless, "the foolish things hath God chosen". Something inside kept jogging my thinking in the direction of the talk the night before.

Bob Ford, a friend who had recently had a fresh encounter with our Lord and was now a committed Christian, was Head of Engineering at the College where I was teaching English. Heads of engineering might know something about library vans! I had tried to contact him earlier in the week.

"I do wish Bob Ford would phone," I muttered to Hugh. Within seconds the phone bell was summoning me.

"I was just cleaning my kitchen windows when I remembered that you'd tried to catch me in at the beginning of the week. Can I help?"

By the following Monday I was asking Directory Enquiries for the number of a motor vehicle assessor recommended by the Automobile Association. Directory Enquiries could not trace the name anywhere. Again "something" inside, independent of the old me, prompted me to persevere:

"But I'm sure you'll be able to help. You see, we are a small group of friends living in Stamford. We want to set up a mobile shop, selling lively Christian books to everyone in the neighbourhood. We haven't much money and we don't want to be swindled."

Quite improbably the voice at the other end of the line leapt into life:

"Well, now I do understand. Hold the line, please." Click. Brr! Brr! Click. "Hallo, caller? I've found you another motor vehicle assessor in Grimsby. I'm sure he'll do his very best to help you."

Only the man's wife was at home. Several hours later the vehicle assessor himself tracked me down in Stamford, not

having realised that such a town existed in Lincolnshire.
There was need now for lots of mutual trust, long distance!
Again, quite improbably, I was game and so was the voice on
the line.

Towards the end of that same week there came his report:
"I'm sorry. It's not on. You see, I went to Louth, drove the
van to the nearest garage with a pit. Extraordinarily, they
knew the van well and had serviced it regularly."

"What sort of condition is it in?" I asked.

"First rate. Cleethorpes Zoo have looked at it and their
mechanic told the owner he didn't want it, only because he
couldn't get his animals through the door."

"I like the craziness. But what's the engine like?"

"Sweet as a nut."

"Then why isn't it on?"

"The body is rust-proof aluminium. There are mahogany
bookshelves, strip-lighting, a swivel chair from driver to
counter-flap. It's all in apple-pie order."

"Then whatever's wrong?"

"You said you were a small group of Christians. You're
not going to be able to raise £390, are you? I can't fault the
vehicle, so I can't get the price down for you. Besides, it does
not have any synchromesh. I don't think you ladies would
fancy double declutching a heavy old vehicle like that, would
you?"

However, by this time we had secured a parking space in a
private car park. We met the following evening, as had been
arranged three months previously, to discuss the pros and
cons of a vehicle versus a building. The fact that £100 deposit
had by now been put by me on the vehicle was not
mentioned. After about one hour's debate, a unanimous
decision was made to purchase the only thing we could begin
to afford: the van, "suitable for chippy or pop-group." While
on holiday the previous summer I had read, "While you were
yet praying your prayers have been answered."

Now we needed, altogether, £1,200 to cover purchase,
stock, tax and insurance. We prayed in silence; wrote on
slips of paper what we could each give, put the offers in a

margarine tub and waited while one of the twenty-two present went home to discuss his gift with his wife.

Would the gifts amount to 50p or £50,000? The slips were totalled while we waited. £1,150 with one to come. He returned, quite unaware of the total so far. Smiling and silent he handed in his contribution.

"Twelve hundred pounds exactly!" announced the tellers.

We all stood and spontaneously sang, "Praise God, from whom all blessings flow!"

Not one of us could drive such a vehicle, let alone maintain it. But quite evidently God was in charge.

5. More Than You Can Ask or Think

That meeting happened in September, three months after Jubilee Week. Only those who had remembered that we had agreed to meet again turned up; only those who were there to commit their time as well as their money could begin to take responsibility for the unwieldy old vehicle we were now to possess.

The first problem, how to fetch the library van from Louth, was solved for us. John, the lorry driver so interested in veteran engines, happened to be on holiday the following week and was more than willing to be driven to Louth in order to bring the van in solemn procession back to Stamford.

"Humph! I see we have fairies at the bottom of our garden," remarked Hugh, as he returned from his day at school and continued about his business in the study. Our children were awestruck to glimpse the top of the old vehicle, settled comfortably by our rear garden wall, and were among the first to swarm over it, to propose tea-parties for the elderly within, jumble sales in our garden for their more gullible school friends, anything they could imagine, in aid of it. They had an instant affection for it, as did all the children who visited it, and they did everything they could think of to cosset the old thing.

"Thing" it could not remain. We had to give it a name. Already we had been given the clues: there had been the talk of foolish things; the Cleethorpes Zoo mechanic could not get his animals in; Noah built an ark when it was not even raining; in my dream the shop contained not only the wisdom of books but solace and shelter for the needy; the ark

had been a shelter; then there was the other sort of ark, the
ark of the Covenant; the stone tablets of God's Word;
books... The Ark!

Christian Book Week had by now become a national
event. Leaflets and advertisements were being distributed by
all the major publishers, encouraging bookshops, schools
and churches to promote Christian books. We soon found
out that Christian Book Week this year began on October
17th, one month and two days after the Ark's first arrival in
Stamford. Very soon the lane behind our house was busy.
Tall ladders were propped against the Ark and people
swarmed over her, painting her a sunshine orange and
cream. A little dove appeared on the front, bravely bearing
its olive branch under a rainbow. Brightly coloured balloon-
shaped notices were stuck on the sides, inviting people to
come inside and see what good things we had for sale:
children's books, greetings cards, gifts for all the family.
There was only one window, the driver's, and a skylight, and
so it was important for us to use these blithe balloon notices
as the equivalent of display windows. Two elderly ladies
blessed us with a novel way of showing that we were closed at
the end of each day: they hand stitched lined curtains for the
cab which showed to the outside world all the animals of the
zoo; from within, when the curtains were drawn, the scene,
whatever the weather, was a clear blue. Our hearts were
warmed at this touch of comfort and love which went way
beyond the practical necessities of preparing a mobile shop.

However, there were plenty of unforeseen difficulties. We
had planned to park the van in the High Street precinct
during Christian Book Week, and quite simply invite the
world in to buy, as cheaply as possible. We had to learn
about the Net Book Agreement (which forbids the sale of
new books at cut prices), trading licences, public liability
insurance, the fact that we had to obtain permission to park
from the Highways Department, the Police, the Town
Council, possibly even the County Council. We had also to
establish a way of buying enough stock, when we had no
trade references and little expectation of placing the

minimum orders that publishers required. We were expected to be both lavish and comprehensive with virtually no capital to act as a base.

Hazel and I had had the chance to browse through the stock we had been sent for the Jubilee Week Book Sale, but now it was a matter of careful selection, for we could not afford to invest our money wrongly: God was in charge of it and we were there to feed the hungry his way. What sort of a buying public were likely to be attracted to the Ark? I spent long hours poring through publishers' catalogues, convinced in my own mind that we ought to buy "good theology". We consulted clergy friends of all the major denominations. I vetted the review of the publication that had received Collins' Annual Book Award. We ordered expensive, large-format paperbacks from Mowbrays and S.C.M. and invited the scholarly to inspect our wares. They had the sense to note what was interesting and to order their copies from the public library... We thought of the friends who were willing to support us by buying. Catalogues from Hodder, Pickering, Kingsway and Lion came to mind.

"Hey, this sounds just right for Bill Burrows. He's always challenging us about whether the gift of healing is available today. Well, here we are: *Your Healing is Within You* by Jim Glennon. Trouble is, the cover shows a woman. We need a bit of he-man stuff for him. One, for trial?' I queried.

"Yes. Read it first,' advised Hazel.

"Six copies of *Joni*? I've read it and so have you. Pat's got our copy now; Joni Eareckson's exciting stuff. What's more, she *doesn't* get healed physically. Interesting." We ordered books on family life, books on the cults, the Christian view of everything from sex to scientology.

Hazel would find requests and orders in the log-book. "What do you know about Keswick calendars? Request here for two tear-off clock calendars as Christmas presents."

"My Strict-Baptist great-aunt had some such thing in the loo," I growled. "But Mrs Noakes is a chirpy enough person. Order three or four more for her friends around here."

"But will they like the price?' Hazel would tap her ball-point against her teeth, cogitating. "Try four." The Keswick calendars were a success; we were rebuked for not having more.

"Key-rings, combs, balloons, diaries, badges, rulers, pens, all with Christian texts. That's what people like," advised a friendly publisher's representative.

Inwardly I quailed. Whatever sort of image would this rubbish give us? Who would be seen dead with Christian texts all over their property or person? Then I realised that here was a world of Christian witness I had never before experienced. Cheap. Cheerful. So what?

The second-hand books of my dream now proved their real worth. We were summoned to fetch a large collection from two elderly spinsters whom we had not met. A maid answered our knock.

"Good morning," ventured Hazel, the bold. "We've come to collect some books."

"We're from the Ark," I interjected helpfully.

The maid turned, and called into the gloomy interior; "It's the ladies out of the Ark!" Immediately she was authorised to thrust several heavy boxes of books into our arms. We were given many hundreds more by well-wishers, and the estimate of how much to charge on each first edition or antiquarian's gem was of vital importance, if we were to steward God's free gifts. The proceeds were to cover some of our outgoings: the tax and insurance, petrol, repair bills, publisher's bills, cost of heat and light... After all, there could be no guarantee that anyone would buy one single Christian book. In fact some of the first people to come in as customers remarked:

"It's all very exciting. I'd love to have that book, but I see you have only one copy. I'll wait till I'm in a bigger shop where they have several." Not good for trade!

The role of the second-hand books as a bait to the general public was even more important. Our balloon notices invited people in, and announced that we had books to suit all tastes. So we had enquiries not only about "huntin', shootin' and fishin'" prints, but also about astrology and witchcraft. Someone even asked whether we had a book on the construction of the ouija board. The volunteer helpers serving at the driver's-seat-cum-sales-counter found themselves in deep water.

"Books on ouija boards? No. We don't sell that sort of thing."

"Could you get one for me?"

"No. You see, it's not our policy."

"Why not? I'd give you good money. It costs a lot to run an outfit like this, doesn't it?"

"Everything gets paid for once we've prayed. It's amazing. And you see, when you mess around with a ouija board you open yourself up to all sorts of evil influences."

"Evil influences? It's only a bit of fun."

"Yes, it may look like fun. But have you met anyone who's been involved for any length of time in such matters?"

"Only one or two people; but they were off balance anyway. One took an overdose. The other was an alcoholic."

"We do have one or two books on depression, and on the occult. I'll show you them. Excuse me if I just pour myself . . . and you? . . . a cup of coffee from this Thermos. It's cold on board the Ark today, isn't it?" The beginnings of what I'd seen in the dream: a search for an escape, Christian concern and real help.

We prayed for the Ark and its volunteer helpers daily. They were, as at the first Book Fair, members of most of the established denominations united as the Body of Christ, reaching out with much joy and friendliness to minister to the needy. But their own human needs were not really catered for very adequately. I do not know what Noah did about plumbing on his ark, but there was none on ours! So the day was divided up into one- or two-hour shifts. October is not the warmest or driest of months. There was a little gas heater on board, but we had only to breathe for condensation to form on all the walls and soak a brown stain into the pages of our new books. The alternative was to have the door constantly open. What use then the heater? The volunteers shared our amateur ways of solving these problems: comparing insights from the Bible in order to help the distressed, giving each other swigs from thermos flasks, advocating the use of fingerless gloves (before they became the fashion of the eighties), passing the word about shopping bargains, giving directions to the nearest and warmest loo. A new way to achieve Christian Unity?

Hazel and I were there as much as possible to adjust the rota, fill in the gaps, help the volunteers. On one occasion when I was returning to the Ark after a lunch break, I saw a large policeman with important-looking chequer-board embellishments on his cap approaching the Ark ahead of me. I ran to catch up with him.

"Can I help? Are you wanting to know something about this library van?"

"Are you responsible for this vehicle, Madam?"

"Well, sort of. Yes, I suppose so."

"Upon what authority are you here?" The town High Street had been closed to vehicles during shopping hours for some time. My mind raced through the list of authorities from whom we had had to gain permission almost to exist, but I could not remember which were relevant. A quick prayer.

"Oh, by every authority, including the Highest." I glanced above my head, hoping the officer would not take me amiss.

"Very well, Madam." He marched off, to my amazement, satisfied and smiling.

It rained and rained that week. When there was no condensation from our breath there was rain from customers' clothes and umbrellas. But again, one of the joys of the initial dream was fulfilled. People came in to take shelter, to browse, chat and share ideas, until it stopped raining.

We were in unforeseen trouble at the end of the week. Our abundant permissions to park in the precinct became null and void on Saturday at midnight. First there was the problem of how to travel with a display of bright new books, many face-outward, to our new parking place. We followed as best we could the practice of the County Library Service and turned the books spine outwards, stretching string and strapping along the shelves. However, some of our children's books were enormous, some minute. They slipped and slid all over the place, as did what we christened the holy hardware – combs, text-cards and balloons.

After shopping hours, Derek, who was officially responsible for the maintenance of the van, went down to the precinct to drive out the Ark. We had had the strip-lighting on virtually throughout the week, certainly whenever it rained. Now, to Derek's dismay, the engine of the van refused to start. The battery was flat. All alone in the dark he realised that he did not even know where the battery was located. At home we were told the bad news from a call box. Word spread by telephone from volunteer to volunteer and there was an instant prayer meeting, courtesy of Post Office Telephones.

Meanwhile, back in the precinct, Derek continued his search. In the dark, empty High Street he peered where he could into bonnet and engine, and poked around underneath. He found nothing, but gradually became aware that he was being observed. With considerable embarrassment he strolled to the rear of the Ark, waiting to be challenged. A car had drawn up; but the occupant was not a policeman.

"Are you something to do with this vehicle?"

Derek huddled deeper into his dark overcoat, knowing that further enquiry would reveal his ignorance about the vehicle for which he was supposed to be responsible.

"Yes. Why do you ask?"

"Did it come from Louth? I was noticing the number plate. It's familiar."

"However do you know that it came from Louth?"

"She was part of the Public Library Service up there. I know this van personally. I've serviced her for more than ten years. Fine old girl. The wife and I were driving through Stamford on our way south. She remembered she had to make a phone call, so we came along this High Street. She's just over there, in the call-box. I've been sitting here waiting for her. Wondered what you were up to, poking around in the dear old van?"

"Well, I'm supposed to be getting her started, but we haven't had her long and I'm afraid I can't even find the battery!"

"Battery? It's just around here, in this little door. My goodness, she's being spoilt. New coat of paint, my old sunshine? And now a new battery. Really smart. Let me help you with your jump leads. Glad I was passing through. Haven't been here for years."

Very soon the old Ark was lumbering along through the dark, wet precinct to her permanent parking place.

We who had been praying had hoped that Derek would be able to find the battery, but to have the Ark's former mechanic sent at that moment to attend to her personally and give extra information for future use was more than we could ask or think.

The place the Management Committee had been offered for the Ark's permanent residence was not the most elegant. Situated near the warehouses by the town's river we were to be close neighbours to an unofficial doss-house used by one or two of the town's more colourful and lively tramps. Also close to us was a lodging-house kitchen whence wafted all sorts of delicious smells our way. The area was certainly not well-lit at night. What was worse for trade was that only those who took a pedestrian passage from the main shopping area to the car-park were likely to discover the Ark at all. So we set about advertising ourselves.

The approach to the Ark was through a deep carriage arch. We decided that the first thing to do was to plaster the walls of this arch with notices. But of course we were soon warned that, since we had no planning permission for this, we could be in real trouble – especially with the owner of the walls concerned. Removable notices put up during the day only would be the answer. We stood in the archway on the day trade began for the Ark, armed with our pieces of hardboard bedecked with brilliantly coloured semi-luminous notices, our hammers and nails and pieces of string, and considered (and prayed!).

This time Hazel and I sensed we were being observed. A gentleman was standing staring at us.

"Having trouble, ladies?"

"Well, yes. We don't know whether we're allowed to put up these notices. But if we don't, no one will know there's a shop down this alleyway. We don't even know who owns this wall."

"As a matter of fact, I do. You won't need too many of those nails. If you look carefully... here... and here... they're really solid, old nails... They'd suit you fine. They're in all sorts of different positions, too. You'll not reach this one up here easily, but it's in a nice, prominent place. Let me hang a good one up here for you. Don't know why they were put here, but they should be useful to you."

Again, more than we could ask or think: not only the identity of the owner and his permission but also his personal, caring help.

We found this to be so again and again. We needed a board on which to display some sort of notice on the street itself, to show that we existed down the alleyway. It had to be something free standing and removable; otherwise we would have again to wait what could be weeks or even months for planning permission. We prayed. Almost immediately, from one of our new volunteers:

"I suppose you haven't a use for an old ice-cream notice board? My mum's throwing one out from her shop because the trade have supplied her with a better one. We don't know what to do with it. Pity to throw it away."

After a few days of rain, someone else noticed that our paper posters attached to the ice-cream board were getting very tatty. She offered to paint out the original ice-cream notice with her own supply of enamel paint and to present us with a really smart permanent sign.

Soon there were more than seventy volunteers on a rota organised by Pat, one of the Management Committee, from nearly all the churches in the town and surrounding villages.

Hazel and I now had one big problem: we had no room in the Ark and nowhere near her where we could sort out card-indexes, invoices and the constant arrival of giant cardboard boxes of books. We explored the whole area. The unofficial doss-house had few windows still intact, and the company there was not entirely suitable... The little window above the Ladies' Waiting Room at the Bus Station suggested a possible room. We stood in the square and considered. Then we remembered to pray. After a little while it occurred to us to consult with a Christian friend who owned a shop nearby.

"No. I don't think that's a room up there. It's just an architectural frill, that window above the waiting room. Of course, I could make room for you above the shop here... unofficially... I couldn't charge rent. You'd have to put up with things. There is a loo and a bathroom. Would you be able to bear having my stock all around you?"

The shop was within fifty yards of the Ark. What we discovered yet again was that there were extra signs of God's love: not just any room, but a clean, cheerful, draught-free, quiet place with the delicious aromas of dried fruit, herbs and honey from the stock all around us, and a treat for all the family at Sunday breakfast – fresh duck eggs. Again, more than we could ask or think.

I began to notice at last that the Lord really does want his servants to enjoy life in all its abundance. He achieves his will not just "somehow", but triumphantly.

6. Life Abundant

I had not noticed it myself, but while all this excitement and change was happening around me, my own personality was being coloured in.

Just as Penelope had delighted in the "firefly" on the ceiling in our Washington kitchen, all creation being new to her, so since my baptism in the Holy Spirit everything and everyone revealed to me a new dimension of delight. I revelled in God's word, shared with him the individuality of each daisy, sea-shell, sparrow; above all, each person, be he or she skinhead, housewife, tramp or television star. He had made me like a little child. Everything and everyone was fresh and fascinating. It became much easier to relate to God and people. In my prayers I did not stop to consider whether my remarks were acceptable to my heavenly Father, any more than a child stops to polish up his thoughts and speech to please his earthly Dad. All I needed to do was to discuss what he seemed to be doing and learn how to join in. Such conversations with God could take place on the side while someone was sharing deep spiritual problems, or while I was all alone in the best and most humble hermitage, the lavatory. It did not matter where or when we talked together, but I found life impossible if we did not. And it became the norm to be able to see how he really was taking notice. He demonstrated clearly how he was doing things – his way.

Even before we had opened the Ark on the High Street there was Tim. A lively lad with twinkling eyes, ever ready to spar philosophically with his twin brother, Tim appeared on all sorts of occasions to help practically with the van, or to contribute to a discussion. One day I heard on the grape-vine that he was to have a major operation. Born with a hole in the heart, he had been operated on as a baby. Now as a teenager he was old enough to take the strain of a major repair. His survival was in the balance: without an operation he could continue warily and delicately, partly living; or he could submit to the shock of this full repair and, if he survived, live fully.

Tim came and shared all this. He had made up his mind. He was prepared to undergo surgery. Would I please "think of" him?

"Think of you? I'll pray for you, too, Tim. If you're not embarrassed I'll spread the word around and you'll get some strong support from the people you've seen in the back lane, refurbishing the van."

"It seems a bit much to expect all of them to think of me. I'll be O.K. And if I'm not, bad luck! That's all, I suppose. But, yes please, do pray for me."

September 14th came, the day that was scheduled for Tim's heart to be patched. The operation took place in Liverpool, miles from Stamford. There was no sensible way in which we could pop in and visit him. There was no clear way in which anyone could find out how things were going.

I telephoned some friends; Hazel telephoned others. Each one we spoke to was asked to contact other praying friends and form a chain. By mid-afternoon Jenny, the friend who had featured in the shop of my dream, radiantly informed me that word had now reached her parents in Devon, who were in turn asking their friends to pray for Tim. By early evening the questions kept returning: how did the operation go? Is he alive? What news have you?

I telephoned, knowing that I could expect the non-committal answer: "His condition is satisfactory."

"Is that Cardiac Ward 5? Could I speak to Sister, please?"

"She is very busy at the moment. Could you call back?"

Half an hour later, I telephoned again.

"Cardiac Ward 5? Is Sister available, please?"

"No, I'm afraid not. We're all run off our feet at the moment. Will you phone back in half an hour?"

Half an hour later:

"Cardiac 5. Sister speaking. Are you next of kin to Tim, Mrs Allan?"

"No, but I would like to get a message through to his mother or father. They are there, aren't they?"

"Yes. Tim's condition is not stable. They are at his bedside now. Is your message urgent?"

"Yes. Tell them we're praying."

"Thank you. Yes. I certainly will. Keep it up, Mrs Allan." Ten thirty.

"Cardiac 5. Sister speaking. Mrs Allan? He's over the worst now. Holding his own."

"Oh, I'm so glad."

"We did have quite a crisis here. It was wonderful to feel your prayers with us. The doctors and I were praying, too. He's O.K. now. He's just opened his eyes; then he stuck his tongue out at me. Must be all right. No brain damage there. But keep praying. We're not sure that he can move his fingers. Mr and Mrs Robinson want to thank everyone down there. It's great, isn't it? Ten and a half hours he's been in theatre."

Next evening Mr Robinson himself phoned us. He had been sent for when Tim was in a critical condition. His heart kept ceasing to function and Tim had "died" several times. The surgeon was now saying it was a miracle that Tim had survived. Mr Robinson and the nursing staff believed that this was the result of prayer. It was later reported that Tim had full use of every part of his brain and body.

God had been doing things his way, quite demonstrably!

Next all sorts of barriers were broken down in me. I had at one time thought it essential to keep up my career as a teacher. My university friends had already reached the upper echelons of their professions; when the children were grown up I should resume my career. Meanwhile, the money I was earning for part-time work was always useful to foot an unexpected family bill, or for treats. But now I was being shown just who was boss. There were plenty of people to take up my teaching work; there was no way in which I

could, or even wanted to, abandon the Ark. So I resigned
from teaching, asking often why I had been given academic
training and personal skill if it was not to be used any more.
It was only much later that I realised how God scoops up,
transforms and uses all we offer to him.

Another barrier was that between Christians of other
denominations and me. In my previous existence I assumed
that the "others" had got their doctrine wrong somehow and
were odd. Now we were together, all revelling in the
adventures on board the Ark, ready to pray with or tease
each other, relieve (or even rescue!) each other, pass on
clothes, do repairs, consult each other for advice. We
learned, too, that what to one of us was junk was for another
a treasure, the remedy to all problems. Typical of this
exchange was Jenny: although her only means of transport
was an elderly bicycle, she was always first to spot a bargain
on market day – the freshest, cheapest lettuces or tomatoes,
or a bulk supply of meat to be shared out as best she could
from her bicycle basket. Last thing on market day we could
expect Jenny to arrive at the Ark with a triumphant smile,
her bicycle handlebars festooned with bulk bananas or some
other perishable commodity that was being sold off cheap.
Such shopping was essential for those of us who had no time
to explore the market and fend for ourselves. The Christian
community that served on the Ark was soon such a real
family that there was no room for divisions and denominations – when several of us knew we would be eating the same
bargain offer Sunday lunch in our separate homes!

Tramps had always frightened me a little, especially if they
were likely to be meths addicts, and it is very difficult to
detect that at long range! Very near the Ark was the home of
a tramp who passed us morning and evening. In the winter
he wore on his head a big, rectangular tea-cosy; in the
summer, a rather battered, but certainly copious, sombrero.
Nowadays he was not just a tramp; he was a person.
However did he keep himself warm? Were the scraps he
scavenged mouldy? Why ever did he not have constant
indigestion? But God was putting real concern for him into

me. Whatever had happened to him to cause him to reject conventional ways of living? Did he need some sort of healing? Did he know Jesus? At that time it was difficult even to elicit a greeting from him. I attributed that to his partially demented, drunken state, originally. After a while I realised that I was still very inhibited and should be much more open in my own approach; I was grieved that I who claimed Christ as Lord could not reach this man who might deep inside have much to teach us.

However, the roaming gangs of skinheads who strolled loudly past the Ark, and occasionally into it, no longer aroused the old hackles of fear in me. Admittedly, we did wonder just how many trinkets and oddments they pocketed as they hung around. But each was a person to be discovered and enjoyed, however many masks of hooliganism he wore as a member of a gang.

We met another kind of gang when we were given permission to have a free "pitch" at the Burghley Horse Trials. These are a high point in the equestrian year. Burghley House, the Exeter family seat, is host to an international throng: competitors, those who come to judge, to administer, to talk dressage or otherwise to display their equine competence. We hoped, somehow, to persuade some to look at what we had to offer, too. So we cleaned down the Ark's weather-stained coat, patched her nose with fibreglass and prayed for Derek as he steered her to her appointed place. When we went to join and "tack up" the Ark for opening, we found her resplendent at the top of an avenue of stalls – sheepskin rugs, Scottish tweeds, leatherwork, Waterford crystal, Garrard's silver, Mappin and Webb, the Ark! What a splendid position, we thought. Incredible. We set out our wares with unwonted confidence and awaited customers.

However, there were those who were more dubious about the matter. Shortly after we had trimmed our display to the best possible advantage, a gentleman accosted Hazel and me.

"Excuse me . . . Awfully interesting place, this . . . I'm not

absolutely sure whether you're aware that there is a slight
snag. You're blocking one of the main thoroughfares of the
show. It's a bore, I know, but I've been asked to move you.
Perhaps you'd be able just to drive her up here and round the
corner? Yes, just a bit behind the main display area; over
there, under that big oak tree out of sight... well, in a more
comfortable location for everyone concerned. Thank you so
much."

We had not yet tried to move the Ark ourselves. Derek
had gone. We gulped and had fellow feelings for the horses
waiting the cross-country race. Just as I was clasping the
enormous steering wheel and preparing to try to double
declutch the gears, help arrived. Mick poked his nose round
the door.

"Looks smashing, doesn't it? What a position, too!"

"Are you willing to move it, Mick? We've been told to do
so. Thank goodness you're a lorry driver."

"Maybe I am, but I've never driven anything like this.
Never mind. Let's have a go."

In no time the Ark had lurched into its position of
ignominious comfort. The oak tree's shelter and the odd
cow-pat suited the veteran vehicle's gypsy appearance. We
felt content. All sorts and conditions of men and women
strolled past and boarded the Ark in its extraordinary
position. The setting was homely; the appearance un-
conventional – an ideal combination in which to meet our
Lord.

The books all these people chose to buy revealed their
joys, sorrows and above all, their fears. We were especially
fascinated ourselves as we observed the number of books
that had been published on healing. However, there were
plenty of sick people who for one reason or another could
not hope to get to the Ark, let alone buy a book. Hazel knew
a Sister at the local hospital, who was in charge of the men's
ward. She enquired whether Sister Coles could use such
books in order to allay people's fears, not only about
incurable diseases, which testimonies in these books showed
could be healed by God, but also about death, which is, after

all, the opening of the final door to life in all its glory. Sister Coles was concerned that the men in her ward (and their relatives) should go out in hope when they left hospital. She chose the books she wanted each to have and personally supervised the assortment we gave her. Under her competent and authoritative Sister's starch there was evidently great compassion, the kind needed for Jesus to work his miracles, both with and without the medical profession.

— With Matron's encouragement we put Ark books in the day-rooms of each ward, to be seen at least by those who managed to get out there to watch television or have a smoke. I was appalled to see how much nervous suffering lay near the surface in those who needed constantly to smoke. Hazel and I could not visit and help all those who were reading Ark books, but we did pray. Gradually we witnessed the fruits in the people we met in the ensuing months, whole and happy about their business in the streets of Stamford, or even on board the Ark.

"Books can get where people can't" was one of Hazel's favourite sayings. The son of one of our Ark helpers was in Borstal; he was fed regular doses of Ark books and began to wish his own life could be transformed.

Dougal, a russet-bearded policeman with an almost unintelligible Scottish accent, patrolled our beat by the doss-house. He often nipped on board the Ark to enquire about a Christian magazine he had first found in Glasgow. Within weeks he had negotiated with his superintendent for a bookcase to be built and Christian books to be given to the station. We were given to understand that there could be no guarantee that the books would be kept in good condition. His colleagues found that the best reading place was the washroom. Very soon we realised just how much these books were being read. There were coffee-mug rings on the covers and well-thumbed pages. Perhaps they were being read overnight in the police station cells, too!

People who, if challenged directly, would normally retreat into their shells or behind their battlements, can take a surreptitious look at a book in total privacy, consider it, reject it, argue against it, pick it up again only to see it still says the same thing, and quite suddenly accept the truth without having to explain themselves at all.

Another idea someone had was to put Ark books on a caravan site. There was an arrangement there that books could be borrowed by holidaymakers. If you wanted to take a book away, you had to replace it with another, new one. A friend of the Ark did just that, on and on!

Two men working in an electronics factory realised that the books we sold were appropriate to their mates' needs: *None of these Diseases* for a hypochondriac, a book on the occult for a secretary who was terrified of the fortune that had been foretold for her, a book on transformed temperaments for a man who found it difficult to control his temper in the home. Both these men listed fifty of their mates, for whom they prayed daily in the lunch hour. They awaited results and many of their expectations were rewarded. One atheist for whom they prayed is now a leading elder in a local church.

Gradually books from the Ark found their way into all the places we could imagine: Borstals, prisons, factories, the police station, hospitals, sometimes schools and old people's homes. And gradually we noticed that those who had been reading were appearing unobtrusively to buy more, or even to offer their own services as volunteers on the Ark.

The establishment of the old van as a shop, the welding together of the community of volunteers, the opening up of new relationships, infiltrating books into obscure places – all this may sound far easier than it was. The Lord was showing us some of what he was doing; meanwhile, with a quiet surge of sinister force, Satan was mustering his counter-attack. It was subtle, evident only as ludicrous pin-pricks at first, but growing in malignancy.

7. The Lunatic Fringe

"Ten per cent of this whole nation actually buys books. Of all books bought, three per cent are Christian, mostly Bibles. The remainder of the three per cent go to the lunatic fringe. They are your retail public." This was the best encouragement someone in the trade could give us, soon after we had begun selling from the Ark.

I was not daunted. We were trying to widen that fringe; in my experience of God's working so far, I could vouch for the impact of the lively biographies and devotional challenges I had come across. The content of our books was perfectly rational, in so far as finite minds can reason beyond the natural.

However, as soon as we had set up the Ark, we met opposition, not only from people, but also from the natural world:

"It doesn't seem to be getting very light in here".
Overheard on the Ark at 4.30 p.m.

Two of the lights in the main cabin seem duff; looking down the mobile, it's the middle one on the left and the nearest one on the right. Also the one in the cab area... Cathy.

Tap dud light strips – and hope. Then pray for a shop!
(Ark log book)

We had survived the cloudy late autumn, but once winter was upon us, the gloom and the rain were relentless. I have developed an attitude of resistance towards the discomforts of a rainy day, the same attitude towards going out in the rain as my mother had had towards the Second World War:

continue living fully and freely; do not let discomfort frustrate you; in fact, do not acknowledge that discomfort exists!

I arrived wet through each day at the Ark, secretly glad to get inside, with a hope of drying out, but:

Please remove plastic sheet hanging over Bible section inside the van, if no further drip there.

There had to be a quick, efficient way of eliminating the puddles on the floor created by drips through the roof seams and particularly through the plastic skylight. We ranged margarine cartons strategically where the rain could ping into them, and dried up the surrounding mess with paper tissues. I tried not to notice just how cold, damp and dirty I was feeling. More important, I tried hard to remove the margarine tubs discreetly every time a customer came on board. All too often we forgot and the inadvertent football game that ensued was cause either for hilarity or apology.

Worse was to come with the ice.

Have we any salt? It's now possible to approach the Ark by the Cresta Run. Phil.

As the winter advanced, cooking salt became less and less available in the town. A spade, hacking away at the shiny black slope from the road to the Ark, chipped off some of the surface ice, but eventually we found there were only gradations of danger, rarely a safe approach, on the various pathways we made.

Plenty of Holy Spirit, but really could do with the Scotch spirit! The more it snows, tiddly pom, The more my toes...

Silently, while the town was sleeping, the snow sifted down and muffled all life. It was easy enough to plod in wellington boots through the town to the Ark, but those who were dependent on vehicles abandoned any attempt to travel. The number of customers was drastically reduced, but so too was the number of volunteers:

Snowy Saturday. In the bleak mid-winter! One light only at 4.15 p.m.

The Ark battery had to do overtime to provide electricity for the strip lights. Like the gas cylinders for the little wall-heater, the battery was heavy and unwieldy, but had to be recharged.

Closed at 4.30 p.m. Nobody around and rather miserable weather. Cathy.

Nevertheless, the shop had to be manned at least as well as any secular enterprise. But one of the achievements of the snow was to bring a thick darkness upon the Ark. It blocked the skylight completely and drifted high onto the windscreen. One day I waded my way through to the snow-crowned van, to be greeted by a note in the log book from a very remorseful Jenny:

Oops! – Sorry, I've cracked the skylight pane nearest the counter, trying to get rid of snow on top, so now we have an even bigger puddle. Jenny.

and the response:

Hence the Ark!

We could feel nothing but sympathy for our ever-cheerful Jenny. Each time she worked on the Ark she got so cold that she had to go and thaw out by standing in the warmth of the heating system in the doorway of Boots; gradually she became able to face the cycle-ride home.

Jenny's attempts inspired me to try to clean the whole roof of the van. I had a small set of household steps and a broom, both of which I could carry down on Closing Day. I was not conscious till long afterwards of the curious sight the roof-sweeping presented. The steps did not allow me to see over the roof. The broom reached only half-way across and I found it all too easy to fling the thing out of my own reach in an attempt to bash at a recalcitrant bank of snow. Then I had to get down the ladder, move it to the far side of the van, grope for the broom and start all over again. While I was unembarrassedly struggling, my whole front coated with snow, a friend of former days was walking her dog, quietly inspecting my activities from afar.

"I'll help you when the weather improves!" she called across the silent, snow-bound wastes. There was a tinge of mockery in her voice. "Lunatic fringe" began to feel too appropriate to me ... A little bit of me wished I was safe at home, warm and dry, an ordinary housewife.

"O clap your hands all ye people, shout unto God with the voice of triumph." It's the only way to keep warm. And Spring's not far away! Takings for the day: £1.71½p!

Spring came, occasionally "bright, with scattered showers", frequently "gales veering" all over the place. The spring teased us, goaded us and encouraged us all at once.

The wind sent the ice-cream stand notice board hurtling down the alley, spun our nail-hung notices face to the wall or under the feet of passing shoppers, and whipped our outside book display off the trestle table.

When the wind was not rollicking around, distracting us from our customers, sudden rain sent us scurrying to cover all outside displays with transparent plastic sheets held down with stones. As soon as the sun came out, off came the sodden covers so that our customers could handle the books. Often the latter emerged damp and spotted – another price reduction... The sun continued to shine brilliantly nevertheless, and there were always friendly entries in the log book:

Two packets of cheese, one for you Ros, and one for Hazel left by Jenny. She bought a big cheese and thought you two would be able to use some.

Oh, what a beautiful morning! Let us praise the Lord!

Pause for thought. Spring must be in the air. Haven't taken so much or had so many in at once for many months – must be my lucky day (will probably rain later.) Ishabel.

But even if the weather was beginning at last to be co-operative, people were being used by Satan subtly and sometimes viciously to oppose us.

The community of the Ark were attacked, especially during the cold weather. With no means of immediate communication, the rota of helpers became almost impossible to organise. Hazel or I filled yet one more of the gaps each time someone failed to turn up.

At that point I felt beset by guilt. We already had our time cut out, dealing with publishers and wholesalers, selecting

books, recording sales and deciding what to re-order. My
family were thrilled and fascinated with the Ark; but only in
as much as it did not encroach upon the time they expected
me to spend at home, cooking, washing, mending, going
shopping with them. Hazel was in precisely the same
position. However, those who reported sick did expect more
than perfunctory sympathy by telephone; they expected
love, practical attention, a personal visit, time spent visiting,
prayer.

The profuse donations of second-hand books were
devilishly a source of sourness amongst us.

*Books (2nd hand) left by Mrs Bunn. Protest – In my
opinion the van floor is being cluttered with boxes of books –
far more than can be used outside. I know we are short of
second-hand book space because of Christmas display, but I
think that less detritus would make a more attractive van . . .*

Many of the second-hand books were offered casually for
sale to the public before the management committee had
checked the contents of each. Volunteers, whiling the time
away between customers, had time to find the odd mention
of lust, or even rape, in one of the second-hand paperbacks.
There followed long discussions about what was worthy to
be sold by a Christian shop: rape was out: were robbery and
warfare in? What about reformed criminals – detective
stories – murder? What was suitable bait to attract the
unbeliever? Often there was a Purge of the Second-hand
Section, which left us destitute of all but pale brown or plum
red and ragged, semi-religious volumes, attractive to no one,
but very respectable!

The changes that had been wrought in us by the Holy
Spirit were making life difficult for some of our friends.
Usually people's enthusiasms wane slowly as they grow
older. On and around the Ark we were becoming more and
more exuberant as we saw prayers being answered and
problems overcome in ways we could not have dreamed of
previously. Despite denominational differences, there was a
strong sense of community. It was natural to talk of the Ark
Family.

But when we asked church-going friends for advice about purchasing premises for a shop, they showed no interest whatsoever, even those who had personal knowledge of what was coming on the market. The most helpful suggestion made was that in our "spare time" we could collect money through running jumble sales. Otherwise the respectable pulled their skirts aside as we passed.

This may well have been because leaders in the town were mystified by the existence and continuing survival of the Ark. Suspicion was rife in both church and Chamber of Trade. Certainly each of the clergy wondered which of his brethren was behind this disturbing anomaly. Few of the town's ministers openly encouraged their flocks to support the Ark, lest it had an alien denominational bias, as yet undetected. Church leaders were mystified by the zeal and dedication to the Ark exhibited by members of their congregations. Hurt that the same enthusiasm had not been shown in ordinary church commitments, some taught that the gifts of the Holy Spirit mentioned in our books were available "only in New Testament times" and advised their flocks to keep away. When we heard of this we tried hard to encourage our volunteers to deepen their commitment to their Lord through their own churches. But the volunteers had been hurt by negative criticism; some found it difficult to answer attack with love.

Denominational differences loomed large within the established churches. People were advised not to buy Ark books "because one of the workers there is a Roman Catholic, a Baptist, low church, high church, Pentecostal . . . and so their doctrine cannot be sound." It seemed to me that the Ark's Roman Catholics were most unfairly persecuted by other denominations, but all we could do was love and pray both for the accused and the accusers, making sure as far as possible to avoid any particular denominational bias in the stock.

We very much needed advice from the local trade about how to proceed as a bookshop. However, the owner of one bookshop told us that we could have accounts with the

major publishers only if we became members of the
Booksellers' Association, and that the Association would
allow only one chartered bookseller in any one town. If we
chose to trade independently we would be black-legged by
all the established publishers.

It took us a long time to get round to praying about all
this. Eventually we did so. Clearly into both our heads came
the idea that we should, as servants of the King of Kings,
consult at the top. We phoned the Booksellers' Association
in London and were swiftly made to realise that all our
information was incorrect.

The only problem we had with the Booksellers' Association was not to do with people; it concerned our premises. If
we ever hoped to become recognised booksellers we must
not only have floor space, we must also have display
windows. No amount of protestation that we had virtually
no window, only a windscreen, would satisfy Head Office.
Again the Ark was an anomaly, something officialdom had
not had to define before.

Once we had established that we could open trade
accounts with publishers as much as we pleased, we were
beset with discreet warnings from friends in business.

Did we realise that we could be undercutting small
tradesmen by selling stationery? (We had a few Christmas
and birthday cards on display in our margarine tubs.)

Had we a large enough retail public to survive?

We did not understand all the implications of these
questions, nor who precisely had threaded such suspicions
and doubts into people's thinking. However there was one
consistent strand of personal opposition.

One of the men who associated himself with the Ark was a
clergyman now in disgrace with his church and deprived of
any responsibility. A man of great personal charm and many
natural talents, he was looking for an opportunity to be of
influence. He was rarely available for the general running of
the shop, but he hoped to be identified as the inspiration
behind the Ark.

With the local clergy informed that this man was under an

ecclesiastical ban, his association with us was, we discovered
later, embarrassing. Worse than that, when he found out
that he could not simply take charge of the Ark and its
volunteers, he began to poison the minds of those both inside
and outside the Ark family with accusations and suspicions
that were devilish. Eventually he started a campaign to
remove the existing management committee and thereby
achieve the strangulation of the Ark. Hazel and I, at least,
were aware of this, but his charm had attracted to him quite a
bevy of support.

There was nothing we could do but fast and pray, which
we did. It requires little imagination to realise that much of
the critical crossfire we received was fairly accurate. That is
why we quailed. I certainly recognised myself as someone
who had bitten off far more than she could chew; and the old
van frequently needed a clean-up; so did my own home; it
did not occur to us to pray often enough; we had not read all
the books we put out for sale, but in the midst of this we were
astonished at the way the Lord provided for all our
omissions even when we did not ask. Amazingly, the next
thing we learned was that the source of our trouble had
chosen to leave the area, ultimately to stay abroad, many
thousands of miles away!

I was astonished how drastically and comprehensively
God had honoured our prayers and delivered us from this,
the most serious assault from the enemy that we had had to
withstand. It was indeed a battle royal in the heavenlies while
it lasted, but the Lord had the victory and the Ark was still
afloat and ready to move on to greater things.

8. "Pray for a Shop"

"Pray for a shop" was our watchword, whatever the problem. Hazel and I kept our "antennae" out, sensitive to any indication of premises for sale. Before the library van was purchased we had found what we thought might be the shop of the original vision. We had mustered our courage and approached the vendors with all we could dare to offer, half the selling price, and we had, as we expected, been sent on our way. The premises had been sold for the asking price and transformed into what became a thriving photo-grapher's shop and studio.

What profits we made by the sale of books in the library van were swiftly used up in the purchase of fresh gas cylinders, the recharging of the great engine battery and in placing new Christian books in the police station and hospital day-rooms. We sometimes had only two or three hundred pounds in the Ark account, although this figure was increasing as we became better known.

We did discover one tiny old house which might be transformed into a shop, if the planning permission were granted. We explored it from top to bottom, redesigning it delightedly, in our minds. The floor space would be little bigger than the library van, but the building was at least cosy and cheerful. There was a minute room upstairs which could be used as a coffee-bar... However, the basic design in no way fitted the original, God-given one and in any case, we did not have enough money to make a responsible offer.

Next door was a shambles. There was a lumbering great building in such disrepair that it was difficult to see what it had been used for most recently. The word "LOCKER-

STORE" was still legible on the masonry at one end; two thirds of the roof was covered in tarpaulin. The large, dark windows were spattered and scratched; cobwebs laced with plaster-dust curtained off any clear view of what lay within.

"Not nice to have as neighbours," I grunted.

"Much better floor space, but hardly any roof – so what's the odds? It's not for sale, anyway," sighed Hazel. We hurried back to the real, friendly world of the old van.

Then two things happened in quick succession. Since people came there to await dental appointments, children their music lessons, others to shelter from a shower, the Ark was a centre for all the news. We learned on the grape-vine that the Lockerstore was now up for sale. The asking price was £11,000.

"That's no good. We want somewhere for free," Hazel declared drily.

"We have got more than we did have in the bank, haven't we? Donations and so on?"

"We need that to pay all these invoices."

I half wondered how we could possibly face another winter in the van. The novelty had certainly worn off. The area in which we were parked was scheduled for redevelopment. Perhaps that whole original vision was merely a pipe-dream. I was not able to face years and years of jumble sales; the book fair had been enough. I was weary. Flat!

Soon after this the treasurer to the Ark, a chartered accountant in the town, called to say that he had received an anonymous donation of considerable importance. In fact we were about to receive £10,000.

Overwhelmed, we realised that we could begin to look around seriously for premises. We were frustrated that we could not write to the donor, and tell him or her how this gift had transformed our attitude. The treasurer himself was unable to tell us more than that the cheque had come from a bank in Leeds. As far as we knew, no one connected with the Ark lived in Leeds. So all we could now do was thank our loving Father and take practical action.

We scurried off to look at advertisements in the local

papers, only to find it was impossible to buy shop premises at less than £30,000 or £35,000. Somewhat mortified, we wandered in to the agents who were selling the Lockerstore. "You can have the key and go and take a look for yourselves. There is nothing you can damage in there – except, of course, yourselves. Be careful of the stairs. There is flooring upstairs at one end of the building; then a steep drop. Just go carefully. Oh, and lock up when you've finished. We don't want vandals in there to add to the mess!"

It was a bleak, drizzly afternoon when we let ourselves in to the Lockerstore. Long planks, a barrow, some old tins of paint littered the floorboards. We could see daylight, not only at the edges of the roof-tarpaulin, but also around the window frames. One of the centre floor-boards had a thumb-hole and we realised that a whole area was hinged. Fascinated, we lifted the hatch and discovered a dark void beneath. A ladder, with one or two rungs remaining, reached down into the darkness. There was also a light bulb on a cable that led right across the floor to a single point in the wall. We plugged the cable in, switched on and were relieved to discover a way of seeing, albeit dimly, most of the building on this wintry afternoon.

Gingerly we descended the gap-runged ladder and discovered a copious stone- and earth-walled cavern, strewn with old lead piping and an office door with a stained-glass window. The old cellar smelt musty with damp and was very chilly. We soon learned, the hard way, the advisability of stooping to avoid the great beams that supported the floor over our heads.

Relieved to return upstairs, we wandered through the rest of the ground floor. The walls were crusted with damaged, chunky white tiles as befitted what had once been a butcher's shop. The rear part of the building was daubed with greasy-looking bitumen. A door with heavy bolts and latch led out to a tiny stone-walled yard. A building adjacent to the yard supplied one of these walls, but its great mansard roof was festooned with slates as ready to fall in the next gale as are pennies in an arcade "shove-penny" machine. One could not predict when or where they would fall. We retreated hastily, trying to make positive suggestions to one another.

"We could grow tomatoes against those walls, anyway."

"Or bring a deckchair and sunbathe. It is totally private."

"We could keep the old van in the back here."

"How could we get it in? Lower it in and out by helicopter?"

The stair-ladder leading upstairs was more substantial than had been the one to the cellar. We climbed it carefully, aware that there was no hand-rail, and only half a floor once we arrived. As we looked along the length of the shop, towards the entrance, we realised that two sets of beams, at different levels, supported the roof. The space between these two layers would not allow a person to stand. However, the rear area had been floored, on top of the lower set of beams, and so I climbed over the upper beams in order to see out of the one window.

"Come on. There's a lovely view over the roof-tops. I love looking down on old roofs."

"I'm not coming over those beams, nor under them. However could we use this sort of space?' Hazel remonstrated.

"Well, we could have it as an office. The beams would keep out the ponderous."

Hazel looked along the length of the tarpaulined roof and I watched a wet trickle descending. She huddled deeper into her green coat.

"I want to go home."

So did I.

But there was no escaping the fact that there were possibilities in that Lockerstore. If we had the roof replaced, we could use the large front area as a shop, the rear part as a coffee bar. It was on the same slope that was in my vision, the windows in the right place to attract my weary lady to see her escapist paperback.

Even if we preferred to "go home" and forget it all, the newspapers would not.

"Peterborough Evening Telegraph here, Mrs Allan. We

have heard about the amazing donation you have received.
Can you tell us who gave it? Have you no idea at all? Come
on, now. You must have some inkling..."

"Hereward Radio. Can you tell us more?"

"Stamford Mercury enquiring. Who is involved? We'd
like an interview."

"Classified Advertisements. We'd like to do a feature on
the Ark, with photograph of the present library van."

Then there were the journalists' interpretations:

"RELIGIOUS GROUP'S £10,000 WINDFALL."

"The blockbusting gift..."

We decided eventually to offer the whole of the sum we
had been given to the vendors. Because payment could be
immediate and direct the asking price was reduced to
£10,000. I and the others involved signed the contract at the
beginning of June. We knew that for the roof to be repaired
before winter we needed another £5,000 by the end of June,
when the builders would start work.

The first thing we did was to take some sheets of scarlet
paper and announce loud and clear:

THESE ARE THE
ARK'S
NEW PREMISES.

"I'm afraid you'll never make a go of that. The roof's in a
very bad way."

"It's in a conservation area. To roof that with Collyweston
slate requires tremendous expertise."

"What about the rates?"

"Moving there? You must be joking. There's no running
water, no gas, only one electricity inlet, no plumbing, no
heating, just plenty of damp!"

"Never mind the roof. Whatever are you going to do for a
ceiling?"

We now had a great incentive to pray and work to raise
enough money to achieve all this and refute the arguments of
the prophets of doom.

9. The Lockerstore

The people who verbalise all one's doubts are those who bring down powerfully the blanket of apathy upon any little flames of enthusiasm that may have started flickering into life. I had seen all the negative aspects of the old Lockerstore that people were now pointing out to me. I was more than wistful about the comfortable life of a part-time college lecturer. The family's needs, the cosiness of being mother, cook and housewife assumed a fresh attraction as, dressed in an old cotton poncho and wearing a protective helmet, I trudged between Lockerstore cellar and scrap-yard, carrying forlorn lengths of twisted piping, valuable to the dealer because it was made of lead.

However, there were signs of new life in the messages now sprouting in the Ark log book.

Richard's plan of Lockerstore can be propped up on the table outside (the van).

Richard, the engineer who had prayed so faithfully for fifty of his workmates in the local factory, and given them so many books, had now volunteered to lead the Lockerstore Work Squad. Each day he was there I turned up to help, I would ask what there was to be done.

"Hallo. Well, I'm just waiting for someone who's good at removing these old butcher's tiles. You can start over there with hammer and chisel, but we really need a sledge-hammer."

"Oh, who's coming with one of those?"

"I don't know, yet."

"Who's offered to come today?"

"No one."

"Have you asked anyone specially?"

"Yes."

"Oh good. Who?"

"God. After that, it's up to him. There's a list in the window of what we need. You've turned up. That's a start . . . of sorts."

Richard knows my limitations, I thought, as tile-chips flew up into my face before it occurred to me to don the protective goggles he had provided. Before very long, he-men from the R.A.F. Station would be relieving me of my tools and muscling in at speed to achieve all that Richard required that morning. They would disappear as swiftly, back to their duty, and would be replaced by an assortment of individuals, each with an unexpected skill appropriate to the moment, and each with an unexpected amount of time to spare, brief or protracted, but often precisely according to the need of the work. Another entry in the Ark log book expressed the faith that united us:

Jesus is coming again. Hallelujah!

And the answer:

What more can we say?

There was plenty more to be said about our worldly situation. It was all like the late spring weather – showery, with bright periods. When I'd signed the contract for purchase of the building I'd felt awestruck and crazy. Almost immediately afterwards we received an estimate for the re-building of the roof: we had to find another £6,787 so that work could begin immediately. I am not a born fund-raiser; all we could do was to make it known that we needed money, hold a second "mammoth book fair" and, above all, pray. Immediately a craftsman offered to make us a beautifully painted collecting box with a "thermometer" indicating our goal. We stood this outside the ramshackle old building and started collecting second-hand books for the book fair.

While the old library van was still trading with spring fervour, the Lockerstore labourers were plying their wheelbarrows and sacks full of rubble. The "family" of the Ark was functioning as a unit: policemen, plumbers,

postmen and plasterers; students, social workers, solicitors
and the "socially inadequate"; airmen, electricians and
engineers, many of the jobless; Catholics, Brethren,
Methodists, Baptists, Pentecostalists, Anglicans and ag-
nostics – the diversity was apparent, but the unity was so
close as to be unremarked by any of us at the time. Richard
produced more and more memoranda:

To organise:
power supply
containers of water, coffee, milk, sugar, biscuits
containers of water, soap, towels, barrier cream
lunch – how many required – volunteers to provide
contact all volunteers
Poster in ARK and at Lockerstore
Transport rubbish skip (Bill Drakes)
Safety gear – shoes, gloves, spectacles, goggles, helmets,
  masks

bricks	*planks (to cover trench, etc.)*
sand	*planks (to get to skip)*
cement	*planks (to go across 1st floor beams)*
weedkiller spray	

Tools required –	*large hammers*	*general tool kit*
(bring your own	*pick axe*	*wire brush*
if possible)	*shovels and spades*	*broom*
	trowels	*dustpan and brush*
	chisels	*rubbish collecting*
	barrow	*boxes*
	large wood saw	

Soon in the Log Book there were entries:
   Kettle given for Ark when work starts and when it opens.
   Assorted glasses and crockery brought in for new
premises, by a gentleman
   Gentleman going to bring stand in, not needed any more
in his shop, to display cards.
   Stand brought in from Richmond's.

Whoever was this gentlemanly gentleman? We never knew.

Mrs Day will provide the washing-up bowl for the bookshop.

Mrs Hibble has left a jar of coffee for the shop.

Little did we realise how valuable this jar of coffee was to prove early in November.

But now it was high summer and the double set of beams were causing much consternation. Bruce, a teacher with a flair for making something beautiful out of junk, was convinced that we should take out the beam supporting the only flooring in existence, that at the rear of the building.

He wanted to lower the floor for two reasons: those working in the office would be able to walk about without bumping into the upper beams; and the lofty coffee bar ceiling would be proportionately lower, so making the room down there friendly and intimate. The only difficulty, pronounced those who knew, was that the beam to be removed supported the whole building...

Measurements and estimates were made and juggled with, but no other solution was found. Bruce and four other able-bodied men set to work. They sawed at the beam; Harry, our architect and friend, retreated to the outside yard to observe developments. Eventually the end of the great gnarled oak beam was fed slowly but with great determination out of the building... A rolled steel joist was inserted through the walls at a lower level... and the Lockerstore stood unshaken. All that remained then was for someone to build in a floor at the new level.

However, even if the Lockerstore was being restored, the old van was getting more and more dilapidated:

The cracked skylight leaked badly overnight.

Packaway table is rather wet. (Ark log book)

The trade grew in volume, as did the number of those involved. Somehow we had to keep pace with the arrival of fresh parcels of books and "holy hardware" and try to provide efficient, attractive, new ways of promoting their sale in a vehicle whose confines seemed to become progressively more limited. In addition its underparts had become a temporary collecting place for blankets and clothing for the Vietnamese Boat People at R.A.F. Swinderby.

The rain had to stop by July, not only to protect all these supplies, but also because we needed a dry summer during which to repair the Lockerstore roof.

July 16th. St Swithin yesterday. No Rain! and the explanation in another hand:

'Cos the Ark in St George's Street is having its roof repaired.

Men were indeed already working on that roof.

Inside, Bryan and his friends were trying to reinforce the coffee bar ceiling. Bryan measured up, deciding that a beam twelve feet long would be adequate to span the coffee bar itself; supports for the kitchen ceiling could be made from odds and ends. He ordered the expensive beam from the local wood-yard first thing in the morning. By midday he realised that one length of seventeen feet across the whole shop would provide far greater strength. We could not afford to waste our first order; there was much consternation. Tentatively, Bryan approached the wood-yard assistant, but his first remarks were forestalled.

"I'm very sorry, sir, but we have only one piece the right size. We haven't cut it yet." He led Bryan to the woodstore. "Here it is. Looks about seventeen feet to me. You wanted twelve, didn't you?"

"No, no!' cried Bryan. "Seventeen feet is exactly what we want after all. I'll take it as it is."

We had yet more need for a dry summer when we heard of the advent of seventy children who proposed to "tour the Ark" as a Holiday Club outing. At most the old library van could hold ten small, well-behaved children, studious Christian mites who loved books. We had neither hope nor desire for that sort of visitation and racked our brains to know however to cope with the rampageous influx we envisaged. We puzzled and worried and eventually realised we ought to pray.

"What if it rains, Lord? All those kids and nowhere to go... Whatever shall we do with them?"

"Workers on the Ark should know who's boss of the weather."

"They won't want to look at our books if it's a sunny day. Anyway they won't have money with them for that sort of thing."

"Put the cheap, jolly bits and bobs outside. You've already grumbled about the hazards of the Lockerstore. The children will love it. They'll use their imaginations and make-believe what it will be like."

The day did dawn bright with sunshine. We set out the tables with our "holy hardware" – combs, note-books, stickers, rainbow-coloured pencils. We festooned the archway with fluorescent notices, stood the battered ice-cream stand near the road and then I set out to find the seventy among all the families taking the sun that sparkling day.

"Seek ye first the kingdom of God," wafted on guitar strings through the warm air and led me direct to the group I was searching for. Anne, their leader, was strumming the guitar; Patsy, her friend, was supervising the children. Little did I realise how much these two were destined later to be involved in book ministry.

Soon the children were bounding off in batches of ten, first to the library van and then to the "adventure playground" of the ramshackle Lockerstore.

It was soon afterwards that I met Jim. He wandered on to the now-deserted Ark, remarking that it was "good to be back after seven years."

"Back from where?" I asked. This tall, sun-tanned man looked as if he'd been on a world tour. Perhaps he'd sailed the Atlantic, a lone yachtsman. Where had he come from?

"Detained at Her Majesty's pleasure."

"Oh, really?" I retained my bright, enquiring smile and surreptitiously checked my means of escape from the counter-seat. "Whereabouts?"

"Wakefield."

Thoughts of jail riots, of rape, murder, robbery with violence slid through my mind.

"Really? What for?" I hadn't yet learned that one should not, in courtesy, ask.

"Arson." I relaxed, not in the least concerned at this moment for our precious books.

"I did £36,000 worth of damage. But it was this book, *Prison to Praise,* that brought me to the Lord. You see, I'm a Christian now and I want to serve the Lord for the rest of my days. Is there any way I can help here?"

"It depends what you can do. Yes, of course, there are lots of ways in which we'll need you in the new shop."

Jim's eyes were sparkling. His face creased into a broad grin. Gradually he revealed that he was gifted – at woodwork, repairing, painting and decorating, even water-proofing, even at a little plastering. He came and helped regularly and reliably in the Lockerstore. There were many times when we wondered just how much, if any, of our rubbish we ought to allow him to burn... but Jim was patient and constructive over repairing and lining the walls of the staircase to the office, cutting little triangles of boarding to fit over the odd shapes and bulges of the old stonework. God's ultimate irony was achieved when Jim was appointed to do the main work of fire-proofing the whole of the Lockerstore!

Our prayer faith was tested fiercely on another occasion. A lady who often walked past the Lockerstore on her way to and from the shops, challenged us.

"How's it all going in there? You seem to be doing wonders," she remarked as she passed me on one of my regular trips to the rubbish skip. "I only wish you'd pray for my arthritis the same way as you pray for that shop."

"O.K. We'll do that. Come on in." We had never been approached like this before. "What's your name, by the way?"

"Olive. Oh dear, I've got arthritis all over me. I don't know what to do for the pain, but I'd value your prayers."

"Come on, up here to the office." Hazel and one or two others were available. Rather embarrassed, we asked whether Jesus was Olive's Lord.

"Oh, yes. I'm a practising Catholic, my dear."

I knew we should lay hands on Olive, but to do this would seem far too official for people like us, more or less novices in the whole business of healing. So each of us, quite casually, almost inadvertently, happened to put a friendly arm around Olive. We prayed, briefly and shyly, then hastily changed the subject and talked about the renovations to the building. It was some weeks before I saw Olive to talk to again. Embarrassed lest the usual local greeting, "Hallo! Are you all right?" should be answered with a negative, I tried to seem too busy to stop. But Olive stopped me.

"Isn't it a lovely day, dear? And isn't life good?" she smiled.

Encouraged, I ventured. "Yes. How are you?"

"Oh, my arthritis? Of course I've not looked back. No aches or pains nowadays, you know."

I had not believed, let alone known. Now I was secretly amazed at the casualness with which Olive was accepting what for me was a wonderful miracle. As soon as I decently could I disengaged myself from the small talk and rushed indoors to proclaim the good news and shout for joy at what our unobtrusive Lord had done.

He had done wonders at the material level too. By the end of June the collecting box thermometer recorded that we had enough money, more than six thousand pounds, to pay for the roof to be tiled with the Collyweston slates stipulated by preservation order, and for the building to be made habitable. There had been an abundance of gifts: money from the second book fair and a sponsored "nonsmoke" initiated by a one-time inveterate smoker; second-hand armless armchairs for the coffee bar (together with a couple of settees), a toy-box for visiting children, hand made and painted with scenes from Noah's Ark by Jim; a collection of mugs and teaspoons painted with an "A" on the handle by the Holiday Club children; innumerable hand-knitted gloves, clothes and dolls; tooled leather bookmarks and keyrings; one or two oil paintings; a gas-cooker, a sink unit, a refrigerator, a formica service bar for coffee, a window frame for the kitchen, linoleum.

There came a day when I felt inundated not only with people's kindness, but also with too much work. I had been home to prepare the family meal at lunch time. When I returned I saw a group of people looking expectantly for me from the chairs in the room that was some day to be the coffee bar. I edged my way out of their sight and upstairs.

"There goes Ros. Ros! Oh dear, she hasn't heard." I hoped they would leave me alone, and go away, but very soon I was summoned back down to be introduced.

"You must meet my friend Robert from Australia."

"Hallo, Robert-from-Australia," I said dutifully. "What are you doing here?"

Robert-from-Australia unfolded himself, all seven feet, and extended a hand.

"That's just what I'm wondering. Can I help?"

"What can you do? How long are you here for?" Standard, often reiterated question asked of all casual helpers.

"I'm moderately good at most things. Question two: twenty-four hours."

"Brain or brawn?"

"What do you want done?"

"Nothing you could really achieve in twenty-four hours. But you could apply your mind to this problem." I showed Robert-from-Australia one of the many problems that caused me to be so shirty with all mankind. The wide, shallow kitchen had been fitted with a plumbed-in sink at the right hand end. To the left of this and well tucked into a window bay was a refrigerator. A gas-cooker with eye-level grill was immediately adjacent to this, firmly piped to the mains and ready to counteract all the efforts of the refrigerator with its own heat.

"We need to get four men to lift this fridge out of the bay, up and over the sink and high over the cooker, to put it down at the far left. Our problem is, we can only get one pair of arms to the fridge in that gap. Can you rig some pulleys or something?"

"You mean you want it picked up, like this?"

Single-handed the giant lifted the refrigerator as if it were a small suitcase, up and high over the cooker.

"Now just show me where to put it." He placed it casually in the right place. "Nothing he could really achieve in twenty-four hours" had been accomplished in under ten minutes. That was why Robert-from-Australia had had to be here, in Stamford, on precisely that day. I have never seen him again, but I hope he may some day read this and realise how much his "brain and brawn" are the Lord's instruments.

10. De Ole Ark's a-Moverin!

October 20th was the Saturday nearest to the old Ark's second birthday and therefore the most suitable for the shop's Opening Day. I heard talk of processions. A concert, even perhaps a party. The whole town was becoming aware that something was going to happen in St George's Street.

Meanwhile, everything in the Lockerstore looked chaotic: men were hacking out the ancient stones and rubble at one end of the cellar in order to make way for a proper staircase to the damp, mouldering rooms down there; the work of laying the floor above the main shop was being disguised with a suspended plastic ceiling; the serving hatch from the kitchen to coffee bar was only in the design stage; a lavatory blessedly would be installed soon; the man who designed the ceiling, David, was also setting up the central heating system; ladders were everywhere, while those who made no pretence to any other skill were detailed to apply paint and did so with zeal, not only on the ceilings, but also into each other's hair and even into Hazel's overall pocket. Those who still endured the rigours of serving on the loo-less library van were unaware of the joys they were missing.

Once the walls were decorated we had to face a crucial question: should we present the would-be customer with really economical, ascetic decor or should we trust the Lord to finance for us something at least a little worthy of the King of Kings? A meeting of all nineteen trustees of the Ark was convened at Hazel's house. Debate was fierce.

"It's a good idea to have something really tough, like industrial linoleum on the floors. That would last a nice long time."

"Yes. Fawn is the best – doesn't show mud and dust."

"I propose carpet. It's more welcoming."

"And gets very scruffy in no time. Imagine ten or twenty people trudging to and fro across that on a rainy day."

"Anyway, we can't afford new carpet. No one's got an old sitting-room carpet as big as the shop floor."

"Certainly not one they are going to give us."

"Lino for me – or bare boards."

"Talking of boards, I've seen a very sensible arrangement of book shelves made of boards separated by bricks."

"But we've observed the shelves in established bookshops and they slope, so that the titles are tilted towards the customer."

"We can't afford anything fancy. It's un-Christian to waste money on frivolities."

"We've got to honour God by doing our very best. What Christians do should be more efficient and beautiful than what the world does, because we are trying to honour our Creator."

"Yes. That's right. God's works are very beautiful –"

"– and cost nothing."

"But he's Lord of the universe. If he wants something done well, he'll provide the funds."

"It's got to be commercially competent."

"There's a sale of second-hand office furnishings on in Colchester next week. Perhaps someone could go and look at that and make a bid or two, if it's suitable," suggested David.

Colchester is ninety-three miles away from Stamford.

"As Ros and I already have our time cut out, perhaps one of the trustees who thinks this a good idea is willing to go to Colchester?" asked Hazel brightly.

The circle of men and women shifted uneasily. There was a long silence. I wrestled within myself. I knew I had no desire whatsoever to go to Colchester. Hazel and I had thought hard and long about an economical, ascetic, shop display. It could be clean and refreshing; it would of necessity be bleak, even spartan; committed, frugal Christians might weather the welcome, but the secular world would feel chilled, even alienated.

"There is something to be said for industrial carpet," put in someone, helpfully changing the subject.

"At what price?"

"Is the Ark suddenly made of money?"

"Are we being responsible, even talking of such things when we have so little in the kitty?"

"Some people get so enthusiastic that they're quite unrealistic."

Silence, now, for Bryan, the Chairman.

"I suggest we pray at this moment, silently, listening above all to the Lord." Bryan bowed his head decisively. Somewhat reluctantly, I followed suit.

"What's the good of praying any more? We've already done this bit before the meeting," I thought to myself. "We've had to trust you all the way along the line for funds," I remarked to the Lord. "So why this sudden economy? What about all the ways you've sorted us out financially so far? Is it wrong to try to make this place welcoming and cheerful? Maybe I am just extravagant... Oh dear. What a muddle. Perhaps you're teaching the others great wisdom about bare furnishings; perhaps Hazel and I have got it all wrong."

Silence. I stared around, truculently, wondering just what special revelation was being given to someone. Then it came, from David, who had recommended the second-hand furniture sale in Colchester:

"The Lord has been speaking to me while we were praying. I realise, now, that whenever he wants to start a new thing he uses new materials. He chose an unbroken foal for riding into Jerusalem – and a new tomb for his own grave. So in order to honour him we should use new materials."

I was mortified at David's utter honesty and humility and immediately wanted to apologise to him.

In no time at all we had agreed to order goat-hair tiles which could be switched around or replaced as they grew worn. The firm we approached had a cheap remnant batch which happened to fit the Ark, with seven spares, for replacements. They were, of course, red. A red carpet for the King of Kings!

Representatives arrived to show us their recommendations for shelving. One turned up on Closing Day. We asked him to drive us into town in his car, so that he could look over the building. As he drove along he asked,

"Tell me. Is this part of a chain store?"

"Why do you ask?"

"Well, there seem to be shops like this springing up all over the country."

"There are."

"Ah, I thought as much. Who's behind it all, then?'

"Whatever do you mean?"

"Who runs the show? Who's the general manager?"

"Oh. Well, he's up there," I ventured, pointing vaguely skywards.

"No, I don't mean him up there. I'm being serious."

"So am I. We're certainly under one general manager and it's 'Him Up There'. He's doing wonders for us."

Among the wonders were the rest of the shop-furnishings: a second-hand, elegant counter, yards of scarlet and light blue curtaining, to be used eventually in the basement, all at a ridiculously low price; two 'Loveable Bra' stands, suitable for holding cards. These Hazel and I were doomed to trundle noisily the length of the Pedestrian Precinct, on trolleys borrowed from the International Stores. Gradually the Lockerstore was being transformed into some semblance of a shop, with an area at the back reserved for later development as a coffee bar. Gradually, too, God's fragmented and separated people were being welded, almost inadvertently, into the Body of Christ, ready to reach out to yet more of the broken-hearted.

By mid-September the children were back at school; early autumn was beginning to colour the edges of the leaves; it was a time of expectation and preparation. Those enthusiastic volunteer labourers, well aware that Opening Day, October 20th was our deadline, were declaring that it should be a day of celebration, which the whole town should know about. We had received friendly but firm notice that the old library van must be moved, because the area where it was parked was scheduled for development. Trade there was slowing down and as the air grew chillier those willing to man the van grew notably fewer. The Lockerstore was still full of debris, resonant with the clamour of drill and saw, plainly not yet ready. Yet the suggestion was being made that there should be a Grand Procession on October 20th, featuring the Old Ark as prima donna, and culminating in the cutting of a ceremonial ribbon across the Lockerstore door. A concert or show should bring the day to a close. The Friends of the Ark were now numerous and so these proposals should daunt no one ... Inwardly I grew tight with apprehension; there seemed no way in which such a glorious day could be arranged. However, the Lord had provided not only these joyous suggestions, but also several competent, practical people who could put them into effect. Above all my attention was drawn to a poster that someone had put up in the library van. It showed the splendour of sunrise and along the bottom were the words, "We are an Easter people and Alleluia is our song!"

At all times of year, even early autumn, we were indeed an Easter people. Christ was in our hearts and he would achieve all that was required for his glory.

There were problems immediately we proclaimed the fact that there was to be a procession: the pedestrian precinct, the library van's most obvious route to the Lockerstore, was closed to traffic each day after 10.00 a.m.; up to that time it was cluttered with delivery vehicles; there was no clear way in which we could make the movement of the old library van into an event; if the Lockerstore was to start trading on Opening Day, then the contents of the library van must be dismantled and redisplayed within seconds of the imagined procession's arrival; could we guarantee that anyone would come? Was the weathered library van's paintwork worthy of a triumphal procession? Who would transport the contents of the cluttered little office above the Health Food Shop? Above all, would it rain all day? Would the library van go ... anywhere?

We had not realised quite how friendly inclined the police were:

"No, Madam, we can't let vehicles through there after ten."

"Can you make no exceptions?"

"You see, the general public are around then. It's not safe for young children and toddlers to have traffic roaring through the High Street when it's an official pedestrian precinct."

"We're certainly not likely to 'roar through'. We're more likely to break down. Your people in Oakham were very kind to us when we did that at Tinwell, if you remember. They kept watch over it on the green there, till we could get it home to base."

"Yes. So we did. Well, we could provide an escort. I'll be in touch ..."

Not long afterwards we were promised the personal escort of P.C. Brackenbury. The very name sounded reassuring and rural.

Geoff, one of the sales representatives, had stood by us from the beginning with friendly suggestions about ways of avoiding expense and with much encouragement about our amateurish enterprises. He arrived from Luton on his own initiative just before Opening Day.

"I've got some free time. Is there any way I can help?"

"Have you any suggestions yourself, Geoff? Anything you're good at?"

"I'll help with your window display, if you like. What were you planning?"

We realised that we had planned nothing.

"Oh, we've a few books that we'd like people to see ... and we have some transparent book props."

"What is your theme?"

"The glory of God. How about that?" It was a sudden

suggestion, but felt exactly right.

Hazel and I found ourselves in a few minutes buzzing off in her tiny Citroen towards the outskirts of the town looking for props. Hazel pulled in by a grassy bank where lay a huge fallen tree branch.

"This'll do. Shift over and we'll let it stick out of your window."

"Whatever do we want that for? It's more than six feet long." But there was no arguing. I huddled under the branch, clutching a bundle of autumn leaves, crimson, brown and gold.

Soon Geoff had draped our window with our spare silky crimson curtain material and propped the books on all the curves and twigs of our branch. The autumn leaves were scattered like jewels. A lesson in window dressing with a difference!

We trundled the library van all round the side streets the night before Opening Day and disposed of its contents into the Lockerstore. It was not until that was achieved that Bryan and a friend discovered that the old vehicle had a completely flat tyre. We saw that matters were out of our hands once more: had we not needed to redisplay the sales material the preceding night, the flat tyre would have revealed itself only in the midst of the procession!

We still wondered about the weather, but could do nothing except pray about that, knowing that the crowds who would constitute the "Easter People" might just stay at home if it rained. October could not promise us sunshine. However, our friends and neighbours offered unexpected help. John, who had originally fetched the library van from Louth, was very glad to offer to drive it through the precinct; Vic, our other immediate neighbour, a keen campanologist, offered to arrange for the town's bells to be rung in jubilation when the procession started.

Still in great anxiety I walked hastily through the blessedly bright morning light of October 20th to the library van now parked with police permission in the middle of the town's Sheep-market – a position that required the minimum of effort for the engine at the start of its final working journey. A ladder was propped against her side. Enormous, bright posters were being plastered all over her and an advertisement invited everyone to follow the van to the new Ark. Bryan had planned a surprise: he had persuaded the children of the school where he taught to do their finest work to honour the occasion and this was the result.

Hazel and the rest of the management committee went inside the now barren vehicle and prayed that the Lord would bless that day, if possible sending the people to do the processing. As soon as we emerged we realised that yet again he had answered our prayers before we had even voiced them. The library van was surrounded by people, several of them from the villages around, many more from the town. They offered to help. Now there seemed to be nothing to do, just for one moment. Then we remembered the office.

In a few minutes an outlandish-looking procession had been formed, the leaders carrying chairs, filing boxes, a portable typewriter and boxes of second-hand books. To our joy, someone had turned up with a piano-accordion. I handed out our own children's supply of tambourines, drums, triangles and bells and John revved up the engine. We began timidly to sing, "This is the day that the Lord has made. We will rejoice and be glad in it." Our voices sounded small. It was as if the Ark was too tiny to face the town in triumph. Our song was to be drowned by uncaring traffic. At the moment when my faith was feeling utterly foolish, there was a new sound on the air; at first it was tentative and delicate; then it burst forth, one answering another in carillon upon carillon. The town's bells romped through the morning air.

As soon as we entered the High Street people stopped in their tracks and stepped to one side. The manager of the local ironmonger's and his staff came out and shouted,

"Well done, the Ark!"

We stopped outside a redundant, deserted church. St Michael's had always been a reproach to the Christian community who could find no use for it. Here, from the steps of the library van, Bryan declared to the general public in the precinct just what the spectacle was about. I looked back along the High Street. As far as the eye could see stretched the Lord's own procession, his people witnessing his achievement. We sang our hearts out all the way. Children swarmed around, some on bicycles; mothers with push-chairs, pensioners, families, everyone joined in, in orderly disarray, to the glory of God, while the bells belted out their triumph.

Richard had trimmed a piece of his cheap curtain to make a ceremonial ribbon. As "manager of the building works", he cut it while Bryan proclaimed:

"Gracious God, we thank you for involving us in the preparation of this building, for giving us the joy of finding that you have a use for us and want us. Now, Lord, we dedicate to you what is so obviously yours. Possess it, dear Father, from basement to attic, through shop, through lounge, kitchen, office and upper room, through corridors and stairs, back room and yard. Use it entirely for your purposes. May it always and only be involved in bringing praise and glory to Your Holy Name. Move out from it into our community and share with more and more folk the love, joy and peace of owning you as Lord, and your Son as Saviour and Redeemer."

And all God's people said, Amen.

11. A Kind of Order

October 19th, 5.20 p.m. Van closed for the last time in Cooch's Court. Tomorrow to fresh fields and pastures new. Hallelujah! Takings: £7.91.
October 20th. Takings: £152.89. Hallelujah! (Ark log book)

We were now certainly an Easter people and Hallelujah came naturally as our song. However, all sorts of new demands were being made on us. One of the earliest log book entries in the new shop read:

A lady came asking if we sold serviettes with religious motifs on. We said not yet, but possibly in future...
The rejoinder followed:

Coming with textual loo paper!

There were many more requests for help, enquiries and suggestions on ways we should expand. However, the Lockerstore was by no means complete.

What was happening amidst all the rubble of the basement was close to my heart. Ever since we started to sell books from the library van I had had a concern for those who for some reason could not cope with a book: not only the registered blind who had access to special libraries anyway, but more especially those who could not hold a book or turn its pages and for those who could not, for the time being, see to read. Hazel shared this concern; together we had attempted to record alternate chapters of *The Hiding Place*. It was an amateurish arrangement, which we abandoned. We could find nowhere totally proof against sound or the demands of our families.

In a completely different context, we both attended a

weekly church prayer meeting. It was here that we had first met Richard, the engineer who had prayed for his mates. As we wandered slowly out of church one evening Richard remarked as he made to leave:

"Well, I suppose I must get back to my studio."

"Studio? Where? What kind of studio?"

"A.K.R. Sound Recording Studios. We haven't got a 'where' We haven't any premises. It's impossible to rent anywhere that is soundproof. It's all in the back of that estate car over there.'

"Did you say, 'A.K.R.' or 'A.R.K.'?"

"A.K.R. It's named after the two daughters of my colleague, John Race."

"Oh!" I was disappointed. This studio had nothing to do with painting, which I loved, nothing to do with the Ark. Then I was given the link. Tentatively I mentioned our own recording efforts and the fact that we had acquired the Lockerstore.

"Yes, I've heard about that. I'll have a look around. There's a cellar, isn't there? That should be pretty sound-proof."

So it was that Richard had first become involved with the building renovations at the Ark. Once he had supervised the structural alteration of the shop he and his colleague, John, were very keen to clear out the rubble from the basement and set up, deep below ground, a recording studio. The stone walls were surrounded by earth, through which water seeped all the time. They cleaned the walls down before coating them with thick layers of damp-proofing solution. I was only too well aware of the suffocating smell and kept away, until eventually I was allowed through the heavy soundproof door to inspect the finished studio.

"Peace to all who enter here" was the poster that greeted me just after I had banged my head hard on a low ceiling beam. Peace there certainly was. After the bustle of the shop and the rumble of traffic in the streets the silence of the newly created studio was stultifying. I recognised our bargain curtain material again, this batch blue and silky. It curved graciously in cushioned padding over the entire wall surfaces. Momentarily I felt trapped in a padded cell.

"A good place to come, Richard, for a rest cure. Quite safe to bang one's head against the wall in here, isn't it? By the way, what happens when we run out of air? Richard? Can you hear me?"

No response. I could see Richard through the viewing panel, tinkering around with all his recording equipment. Then, to my relief a loudspeaker connection crackled. "Enjoying yourself in there?" grunted Richard through the viewing panel. "Come round and in here and I'll show you my drum machine."

I went into a tiny room festooned with switches and machinery. I was completely baffled by talk of a sound mixer, a half-track stereo tape deck, a four-track tape deck, a noise reduction unit, three cassette decks, reverberation units and a drum machine.

All this was in vivid contrast to what was happening both in the rest of the basement and also in the area being made into a coffee bar. In the studio there was silent competence; everywhere else was noisy, even shambolic.

The room adjacent to the studio was being made into a Quiet Room. The crimson curtain material had been made up into two ceiling-to-floor curtains by a lady from the Salvation Army. The carpet had been provided from an Anglican sitting-room and fitted by an ex-member of the Closed Brethren. The fire and surround had been bought in a sale room by Jenny from the Free Church. An air pump was being rigged up by a Methodist. The room had been decorated by "Alleluia Mick" from the Pentecostal church. A wonderful combination of people were making the room a real haven.

Early in November our improvisation skills were put to the test. One rainy Wednesday morning an elderly lady arrived from Bourne, thirteen miles away.

"I've come to sample your coffee, dear. Whereabouts is the coffee bar?" I stood in the archway which separated the shop from what at the moment looked like a second-hand furniture dump. Assorted armless armchairs and a carpet were piled at one end, while we waited for the cement on the floor to dry out. Chunks of wood and strips of plank permitted access to the kitchen.

Hazel whisked out an upright chair for our guest and placed it by the counter. "The coffee bar isn't quite ready yet. I mean, it's out of order, today. But do sit down here. We'll bring a cup through for you." I had slid out into the skeleton kitchen area and switched on the electric kettle. We were always able to have a quick drink since we had been given that. We had been given a jar of coffee when on the library van; the Holiday Club mugs and teaspoons could now come into their own at last. Soon there was a satisfied entry in the log book:

I was privileged to be served with the first cup of welcome coffee – November 7th, 1979 at 11.15 a.m. Glory be! Estella M. Male.

The coffee bar, once complete, became a meeting place for everyone who needed a chat and a rest during a shopping expedition. Coffee, tea or soft drinks and biscuits were available free of charge, but the donations we received in the cat-shaped money box, the Kitty, paid not only for the drinks but also for our office stationery and postage. Friends gave us a steady stream of second-hand secular books to display in this area, in order to attract the casual customer and so fulfil the original dream. They also gave the fruit of their skills: they knitted, carved, painted, made dresses and cooked, all so that God their Creator could be glorified in the coffee bar.

However, there was a snag. The coffee bar had developed a certain air; with its clean but worn armchairs, selection of second-hand books, Tear Craft items, hand-made products for sale and above all its fingers of shortbread cooked specially for the Ark by Richard's Italian wife, it had become an eccentric rendezvous for the gentry. The Kitty benefited, but Hazel and I knew that this was not the clientèle for whom the coffee bar was designed. Conversation was carefully groomed, and banal, leaving no room for admission of failure or sharing of delight in the Lord.

Then Josephine, Richard's wife, solved our problem unaware. She had three children under five years of age; she was now expecting her fourth; she declined to produce any more shortbread. It was early on Friday morning, the busiest day in the Ark, that I realised.

"I can't offer them bought biscuits, Lord. They're dreary."

"You have the materials to make something. Just weigh it all into bags and take it with you."

Reluctantly I obeyed. As I freewheeled on my bicycle to the Ark I met Muriel.

"Hello, Ros. I'm on coffee bar duty. Your Friday morning special!" she grinned.

Once Muriel was established, with kettle on and mugs arranged, I presented her with my plastic bags. "Just mix that up, if you have a moment, can you?" Muriel looked dubiously at my offering. She retained her helpful smile and launched into this act of creation. I went up to the office to help Hazel sort out a huge crate of "holy hardware" so that she could start burning the accompanying wood shavings in the back yard.

Soon there was a cry up the stair-well.

"I've put the biscuits in but the oven's not hot. There's a big smell of gas."

"You need matches, Muriel."

"Oh, I thought it was self-igniting. That's O.K., then." I heard the sound of the coffee bar clientèle arriving; at the same time I smelt singed hair. Muriel had indeed lit the oven and her eyebrows, too.

"Ros or Hazel! There's a fire in the back yard."

"Yes, we know. That's all in order," floated distractedly from the office. Ten minutes later I smelt burnt flour.

"Are Muriel's biscuits all right?" I whirled through the coffee bar and whisked a smoking black and tan collection out of the oven.

"Sorry about that," grinned Muriel. "Better luck next time." Through the acrid haze she committed another batch to the oven and I returned to the office. Hazel and I settled

down to a concentrated time of work, determined to clear
the debris of packaging and to take into the shop the new
display of goods.

"Ros or Hazel, there's a fire in the yard."

"Yes, we know."

"Did you know it's now three fires?"

In time of fire, always remain calm... One at a time we
sauntered through the shop and the coffee bar, as if to go to
the cloakroom. Once there we hurried. I glanced at the fire
extinguisher we had been given on extended loan, to be used
only in real emergencies. Instead I grabbed a milk-jug and a
tea-pot full of water. Hazel had a saucepan.

Outside, there were indeed three fires; our spare beam and
board supplies had caught. Jenny was lifting the third fire
with a spade.

"Are you trying to let the air in, to encourage that, Jenny?"

"No, I was just spreading it around so that it went out."

"That way, you'll start a fourth fire."

Hazel sloshed on her saucepan of water: I stood dribbling
my teapot with one hand and throwing the jug-full with the
other, in full view of the coffee bar. I felt very silly.

However, whatever public image we might have had at the
beginning of the day had already evaporated. The coffee bar
had suddenly and completely emptied. As I received the full
force of Hazel's mockery for my failure to use the fire
extinguisher, I realised that our prayer for the coffee bar
clientèle to be changed had been answered.

Now we must pray for the lost and lonely to come in and
join God's family. Sooner than we could have imagined they
came. A surge of skinheads sauntered through the shop
jostling the other customers and apologising mockingly. I
gulped as I saw an elderly widow move her shopping to make
room for them. As she in turn scolded and teased them, I
heard one mutter: "She's all right – a good li'le ole girl, really.
She's Pete's ole dear's mum."

It was a long time before I dared venture amongst this
crowd. I was fascinated by the different multiple ear-ring
styles. Gradually those who had grown more hair cheered

the colour-scheme of the coffee bar with burgundy broom-heads, emerald ear-muffs and cochineal crests. I tried to persuade what men turned up among the volunteers to go in and chat, to run a discussion group, even to introduce them to Jesus.

"Humph! I haven't got time today."

"I've really come to decorate."

"Why not get some of these fellows to help?"

I nodded towards the assortment of youths taunting each other, guffawing, withdrawing behind spotty masks.

"You ask them."

"Shut up. Ere comes Melons." I was standing near the counter, by the coffee bar entrance.

"Wotcha, Melons!"

"You shouldn't allow them to call you that," remonstrated the assistant.

I looked down at my rather tight-fitting T-shirt and realised at last that I was being greeted. With hilarity and relief I greeted the blond, spiky-haired girl-friend of the youth who had greeted me. He had introduced her earlier by his own nickname.

"Wotcha, Ratbag!" I grinned. I was in. From then on, I had no fear of these lads. Several of them did help with the decorating, occasionally larding gloss paint over the basement stair walls and delicately picking out the woodwork with emulsion, but they were witty and willing.

Every so often one or another would disappear. Our clientèle became subdued.

"Where's Pete? I haven't seen him for weeks."

"North Sea Camp." This came from Neil, a hollow-faced, relatively quiet lad.

"Whatever has he been up to now?" I was angry.

"Drugs. He's lucky. Short, sharp shock. Better than remand at Lincoln and not knowing where they'll send you." There was an anxious look on Neil's face.

"Going to court on Wednesday myself." He giggled nervously out of the window.

"You are, Neil? What have they got you for?"

"Breaking and entering. But I didn't take nothing. It was my mate that took the stuff. I just went for the laugh. Will you be coming, Wednesday?"

"Who, me? To court? Well, yes, of course."

I spoke as if it was my constant habit. Someone inside me was telling me I had to stand by these lads, whatever they had been up to.

A family of three came to inhabit the coffee bar. The father, a second Richard, different again from our engineer friend, was the most assiduous in coming. He would sit reading in a corner at first, reading everything he could lay hands on. Then, he became absorbed in a second-hand Bible. Soon his wife joined him, together with their son Adam, strident and boisterous, harnessed down firmly in his high pram. Richard and Stella would sit through the drizzly November days, hunched sadly together and reprimanding Adam every time he demanded to get down from his pram and play with the cars in the Ark toy-box, hand-made and painted by Jim, the ex-arsonist. Each day the sad little trio would make a hasty exit at about 3.30 p.m. in order, we soon learned, to retrieve two older children from school.

One day Richard came upstairs to the office, with Stella somewhat bedraggled, closely in his wake. He said that he had now committed his life to Jesus and wanted Stella, who did not read much, to do the same. We sat them both down. Stella seemed to be quietly hopeful, even excited, as we discussed with her what was involved. Hazel and I were uncertain just how much she understood, but she was childlike in her desire to be like Richard and put her trust in Jesus as Saviour and Lord. So we prayed for them both. I noticed a new bounce in their step when they left, to retrieve Adam from his coffee bar baby-sitter.

Only a short time later, we received another office visit. Richard and Stella had decided that they wanted to get married.

"We certainly would if we could. Trouble is," sighed Richard, "Stella wants a proper big wedding she'll remember. We can't possibly afford the kind of wedding she wants."

"Why don't you let the Ark do it?" I blurted out expansively.

"Yes, why not?" confirmed Hazel.

"Yes, and you two be the Best Man," suggested Stella eagerly.

We were disconcerted. "Er, both of us? Best *man*?"

"I haven't got a hat."

"Nor have I."

"No, we won't do. You'd better rake up an old friend to do that. But we'll have a go at the rest."

"And between us we'll be bride's mum," I volunteered, remembering that Stella's parents had died while she was a child.

An embossed, silver, comprehensive wedding invitation arrived. It was addressed to "All our brothers and sisters in Christ" and embraced everyone at the Ark. Nevertheless the ball was put firmly in our personal court. On the inside flap were the words: "For the glory of Christ, we live in his name. R.S.V.P. to Ros or Hazel."

There were many crises. We had the offer of a cake made specially by an R.A.F. chef. Stella wanted red, white and blue sponge; the chef insisted upon rich fruit cake with royal icing. Stella's older children were to be bridesmaid and page-boy; neither they nor the rest of the family had appropriate clothing until the usual "Wanted" list appeared in the Ark. The Best Man, Stella's brother, thought he would be unable to turn up on the day and so an R.A.F. Ark volunteer was nobbled for the occasion and has remained a staunch friend ever since.

Gradually the Lord welded the day together his way. There were hand-made matching velvet outfits for the children; someone dressed the church with flowers; someone else dressed both Richard's and Stella's hair for the occasion; an aerial photographer from the R.A.F. was on hand, at ground level; the guests, nearly all Ark people, each brought rare delicacies to provide an enormous wedding breakfast; Stella's former Sunday School teacher, now an elderly farmer some distance away, donned a top hat and fathered her through the ceremony; the bride arrived driven by my husband in our well-valeted, if rusty, silver Fiat bedecked with white ribbons; the minister taught them and guided them through the service. As I wrestled with Adam on my lap in his new romper suit, in the front of a packed church, thanksgiving welled up within me. Christ's body was united together yet again in ministry and worship.

Stella still has her bouquet to remind her of their commitment: a tiny hand-stitched array, made of silk, specially designed to last...

12. Ministries of Healing

A kind of order had now been established in the Ark, in the coffee bar, shop and studio, and the Quiet Room was in use for a great variety of people: it was used as a private rendezvous for Ark helpers in need of a little peace and privacy and, increasingly, for counselling and prayer for Christ's healing.

This matter of healing and counselling became personally important to me. I wear contact lenses and was experiencing considerable distress in my right eye so that when I wore the lens the whole area near my nose was sore. Moorfields Eye Hospital in London diagnosed a mole near the iris, "probably malignant". I watched the specialist drawing his diagram in my file. I could not see, upside down, what he was writing, but I could see what looked like a spider drawn near the circle of my iris.

"We should excise this fairly immediately," he remarked as he finished his sketch. "It is likely to invade the iris."

"Does that mean hospitalisation?" enquired my husband, Hugh. "In this hospital?"

"Well, yes. Your wife will have to keep her eyes absolutely still for about ten days."

My mind raced. My only occupations when alone and ill in bed were reading, writing and sketching. Then I remembered our new tape ministry.

'Couldn't I be operated on in Peterborough?' I pictured friends bringing an inexhaustible supply of first-rate tapes.

The specialist hesitated. I explained who the local eye surgeon was. "Oh, yes. We know him well. He's excellent; he trained with us. I'll write to him immediately because this operation is urgent."

Much relieved that I was not to be cut off from all the family, including the extended one at the Ark, I set off for home to await developments. Days passed. Nothing happened. Christmas drew nearer. My heart rose up in gratitude; unless it was all very urgent I might be allowed the joy of Christmas at home. Weeks passed; the Post Office strike, which had made the sending of Christmas cards much more difficult, was now ended and we were into the final run-down to the great Birthday.

Hazel and I used to take Ark books to Trevor Dearing's Power, Praise and Healing meetings in the local Methodist church. It was our habit to sit near the bookstall in the foyer at the rear of the church during these services – partly so that we could be of some help to late-comers or early leavers, and partly so that we could get to know our stock! The sermon had come to an end; the sick were queueing in the aisles in order to take part in prayer for healing.

"Aren't you going about your eye?"

"Just about a tiny mole?" I thought of the cancers, paralyses, even blindness that others were suffering from. "No. It's too insignificant."

"As you please," shrugged Hazel, turning to another book. "If you don't believe Jesus can heal... that's not my business."

"Don't believe Jesus can heal"? I thought. Whatever next? Indignantly I rolled up my spiritual sleeves and set out on the long walk to the front of the church. Still I was plagued with misgivings. What was troubling me was piffling, compared with the suffering I saw around me. Then I remembered that I had been asked to pray for a close relation who had inexplicable lumps on his chest.

"I'd like you to pray for my second cousin. He has lumps on his chest... and while you're about it, please could you put in a word for my eye. I have a mole on it. It's invading the iris, I believe."

"Malignancy, we curse you, in the name of Jesus." The minister passed a finger lightly over my eyelid and pain shot through me. Tears flowed freely down one cheek as I fumbled my way in embarrassment back to my seat.

"Fat lot of good that was!" I snorted, as I removed my contact lens to relieve the pain. "Now I'll have to sell books one-eyed." I felt flat with disappointment and was glad to bury myself under the blankets as soon as I arrived home.

Next morning I got up and washed. Gingerly I put in my contact lenses, fully expecting the usual ache to establish itself around my nose.

I had no pain whatsoever.

As the morning, afternoon and eventually night came, I realised I had been healed!

Soon after that, during a routine visit to the local eye-specialist with our elder daughter, Juliet, I discovered that, thanks to the Post Office strike, Moorfields' letter had never reached him. It was now only a matter of days before I was in his chair under the glare of ophthalmic equipment. The mother of one of my son Rupert's friends, Esther, followed as a student in his wake. She acknowledged me discreetly.

"Humph!" The specialist stood back to let Esther peer down the optical microscope. "You have here what looks like an accumulation of pigment, Mrs Allan. Nothing whatsoever to worry about." He turned to his student. "No sign of radials, are there? We'll just take a photograph of this and ask you to return in six months. There should be no change at all, if I am right."

The following weekend, Esther was ensconced in my kitchen, in order to collect her son from playing with ours. I introduced her in her student guise to my husband.

"Hugh, meet my ophthalmologist, Esther. By the way, Esther, what would that blob on my eye have looked like if it had been a malignant mole?"

"Oh, quite different. You would have been able to see the roots radiating out from it, just like a spider's legs." I remembered my upside-down view of the Moorfields surgeon's spider and pondered ...

"Then I have been healed!" I declared. "You see, after Moorfields diagnosed a malignant mole, I went for prayer for Christian healing."

Esther made no comment.

Six months later my eye was again under the specialist's microscope.

"Yes, as I thought, this is merely a collection of pigments. Will you be seated again." He resumed his seat at a desk and started to write. "You have nothing wrong with your eye. I can discharge you." I had resolved that when this happened I would give God the glory for what he had done in me. Now that did not feel at all easy. The darkened room was entirely silent except for the slight rustle as the surgeon scribbled his notes. I cleared my throat.

"I ought to tell you: I have had Christian prayer for healing since going to Moorfields."

Again, a total silence; this time the specialist's pen was poised.

'We'll have you under the optical microscope again, please." He scrutinised my eye. "Yes; just an accumulation of pigments."

"What about Moorfields' diagnosis?"

"Moorfields made a mistake," was the muttered response ...

While I concentrated on the skinheads and court cases, others needed help. The volunteers themselves were at various stages of distress or commitment and joy, but there was a steady stream of Christian friends of all ages and backgrounds as the backbone of the coffee bar clientèle. They weathered the jibes of the gangs of youngsters, recounted amusing tales of their own walk with the Lord, reached out with concern to the sad, and were quite evidently filled with praise whenever they heard good news.

One or two of the deeply depressed found solace just sitting quietly in this atmosphere. Dave, a law student, had dropped out of University, dropped out of any hobby he had ever pursued, dropped out of friendships, dropped out of living. Imperceptibly he started to listen to conversations around him and even to chuckle at the naive incompetence of a lad, newly committed to the Lord and trying his best to help in the shop. Soon he had made an undemanding friendship with this young man. Together they explored Scripture and their relationship with Jesus. Now Dave, completely healed, is able to help run a Christian bookshop himself. On the other hand, Reuben, also deeply depressed, spent hours sharing his career and family problems and eventually committed suicide.

The whole matter of prayer for healing was brought sharply into focus during and after Trevor Dearing's ministry in the Ark basement. Hazel and I enjoyed being Trevor's aides, even in the matter of popping along to the nearby Co-op for another bottle of olive oil to be used in the ministry of anointing. We often had not only to supervise the appointments register, but also to be in attendance during the ministry.

My agnostic aunt, Penny, came to see me from London, one day. As I drove her to our home she remarked upon the excruciating pain she had in her right arm.

"The tendon has come out of the sheath, I'm told. They can do nothing for me – and nor of course can I! Can't even brush my own hair. I haven't had the use of it for over nine months. Could you be a darling and put up one of your arrow prayers? Your mother tells me you have a hot line."

I knew that I had no hotter line than anyone else, and growled, "Why don't you ask him yourself?" Then I felt remorseful. We were passing the Ark. "That's the bookshop I'm involved in. Hang on a moment." I drew the car up on the pavement. The Ark was closed, but I had a key. "Now what am I supposed to do, Lord?" I knew Penny wouldn't want to come in; but I found myself running in and grabbing the first book I thought of: Trevor Dearing's *Supernatural Healing Today*. I jumped back into the car and tossed the book into Penny's lap. "Present for you," I muttered in embarrassment and roared off up the street.

A day later Penny had read the book and hated it. Two

days later she had reread it. Within four days she had made a special "emergency appointment" with Trevor just before his departure to St Luke's, Seattle, and had emerged fully healed, whirling her arms round and round and praising her Lord.

Someone had remarked, "We don't know what we'll do now you're going to the States, Trevor."

Trevor's response was: "Perhaps you'll all get on with the healing ministry yourselves."

I soon found I had no option but to trust the Lord to do his stuff, however feeble the prayer instrument. The Christian Families Conference in Canterbury had taught me that we were all here to get on with the work the Holy Spirit gave each of us to do. If we were given compassion for someone in distress, then we must have the courage to reach out to them in faith, and ask the Lord to do the rest. I had worried when I heard that great preachers like Jean Darnall used olive oil when praying for healing. Immediately afterwards, on the Conference camp-site, I was called upon to pray for the daughter of a friend. We had only cooking oil, which was poured lavishly all over the poor child. Next day, someone crippled with a knee injury privately asked for prayer. Now there was only solid Trex available! Both the child and the adult were healed, just as indeed had the others who had not been anointed at all.

It was in a local chemist's shop that I met a friend, Caroline.

"Whatever have you done to your wrist, Caroline?"

"Oh, I've got it strapped up like this because of my appalling arthritis. It's rotten, really, because I can't get on with my painting – and that's my livelihood. You'll have to make me an urgent appointment with Trevor Dearing."

"I can't. He's out of the country."

"Well, you and Hazel will do. Are you going to be in the Ark in the next half hour? I'll be right along." With that she left the shop and it was my turn to be served.

"Stand by, Hazel. Caroline's coming in any minute for

prayer for healing. We've got to do the praying."

"Don't be stupid," growled Hazel. However, she packed away her papers and led the way to the Quiet Room. Soon Caroline appeared. In complete trust she volunteered, "I ought to confess any evil that I've been involved in before I can be healed."

I gulped. "Go on, then."

"I've used the Black Box."

"Whatever's that?"

"Oh, you know. You send a hair or a toe-nail clipping to the man with the Black Box – plus some money, of course, and he does his stuff."

"What stuff?"

"Something or other with a pendulum... and I renounce the whole lot, in the name of Jesus."

Caroline seemed to know much more about what one did on these occasions than I did. All we had to do now was to ask the Lord to heal her. As soon as that was done, we each went back to our work and did not mention the wrist again. It was at an event much later that I learned that something had happened to Caroline that day. She volunteered publicly to proclaim that she had been healed by the Lord. She raised her arms in praise and wiggled her one-time arthritic wrist in every direction.

Meanwhile I myself was awaiting God's answer to my anaemia, which had become so acute that the doctor had recommended a hysterectomy, to follow an urgent course of iron injections. I had asked to be allowed to give the whole matter a year – and I had secretly challenged the Lord to heal me in that time. The final date arrived, and I made an appointment to see my doctor. The blood-count was still very low and I was sent to a gynaecologist who announced that I needed an emergency operation "as soon as I could face it."

"I'm willing to go into hospital as soon as you wish," I agreed.

"Do you mean to say you're not frightened any more?" I

was baffled, but gradually realised that my private arrangement with the Lord had been interpreted as a delay caused by fear.

During this time I had come to know Margaret. She had arrived in Stamford from the United States, with her seventeen-year-old son. As she and her son came more and more to help in the Ark, I learned that she had been through a difficult time while abroad and had returned to her home town here, divorced and anorexic, but still with a calmness and wit that I understood and warmed to.

On December 24th, 1980, she appeared amongst the customers in the last-minute Christmas Eve rush. Eventually I greeted her and asked if I could help.

"Are you looking for something in particular?"

"No, thanks. I'd like to have a private word with someone."

Upstairs in the office Margaret, dazed, sat down gratefully and blurted out some of the details of a devastating disaster, in which her own daughter, still working in the United States, had died. Margaret had been brought the news in Stamford that day, and had wandered into the Ark, without even knowing why.

Once Hazel had joined me, we groped around for ways in which we could help. I had my own "qualification", Penelope's death; Hazel had her personal tragedies, too, but the circumstances of both were intimate and relatively gentle. We all three stared hopelessly at the carpet. Tentatively, I offered to pray; Margaret did not respond very positively, but we knew by now that prayer was the effective tool and so we asked our heavenly Father to put his arms round Margaret; that he would help her to understand something of his purposes in all this; that something good would come out of evil.

Margaret just huddled deeper into her winter clothes, numb. The excited hubbub of Christmas Eve late shoppers welled up in the background, an ironic comment on this, and reminiscent of the appalling way in which the world had continued about its bland business during the hours just after Penelope's death. I did not realise, then, that this also was the beginning of Margaret's search for a new relationship with God.

At the beginning of the following month I had my operation. As soon as I emerged from hospital, I was able to appreciate a new dimension of Margaret's anorexia: she loved cooking and had committed herself to providing for me. So each day she would arrive with a bag full of delicious, health-giving concoctions. She would make sure that there were no heavy chores for me to do, and would sit on the hearth-rug, savouring my delight as I ate. That was a little disconcerting; soon afterwards she would stalk off in the January drizzle to eat raw cabbage. My own doctor, when she visited one day, remarked, "Anorexia nervosa is easy to diagnose – and a devil to cure." It was only at that challenge that I began to realise that there was a case for really militant prayer. Margaret brought her hand-beaten silver jewellery to show me one lunch hour. She had designed and made it herself. Together we admired the beautiful gems, polished and refined in the jostle of the polishing drum. I pictured Margaret as one of these, a jewel encrusted and damaged by the oppressions and hurts of life and needing to be purified and honed by the master jeweller.

Many months later, Margaret was to interpret for me a mental picture we had been given. In this I was trying to come out backwards through the doorway of the Ark, but was obstructed by what I was carrying and cherishing in my arms, a model of the bookshop itself. I was indeed at another turning point in my own life, from which I was to be led, out of the Ark, and on into a new adventure with the Lord.

13. XLU – Christ Loves You

I was sitting in my chair by the fire having my nap. For several weeks after the hysterectomy this seemed to be necessary. The fire stirred a little; the drizzle fell against a grey backcloth outside.

And I was in a helicopter, a simple, toy-like craft, with wooden propellers. Beneath me the fields stretched in a patchwork of gold, brown and green; horses, cows, sheep were set out, almost like a model farm; the spring air was brilliant with light.

Bouncing along between the hedgerows was a white mini-van.

"That's good! Rupert would love to have that." Our son was too old to be playing with toy cars, but he still collected Matchbox models to preserve as antiques "for his children's children".

The helicopter pilot immediately reduced altitude so that I could see what was painted on the side. Beneath a rainbow were printed the words, "Christian Book Service". I had always felt stifled by the Ark's respectable sub-title, Stamford Christian Book Centre; my heart leapt at this new wording.

"Christian Book Service. Service: I like that!"

Suddenly I was in the tiny van, driving it. We were arriving at some houses. On the right were grey stone cottages. People were emerging from their homes, hurriedly whipping off aprons or changing from their gardening boots, forgetting their curlers in their haste.

However, we had drawn up outside a very different establishment. On our left was an open-plan estate with spacious lawns sweeping down to the road. Through a picture window I could see two or three well-groomed ladies.

The expression of one, who was arranging meringues, suggested, "My dear, have you seen what's drawn up outside? Is this really what you expected?"

Embarrassed, I climbed out of the driver's seat and walked to the rear of the van to see just what we had come in. I opened the two rear doors; inside were many boxes of books. I stood back in despair, aware of the helicopter pilot behind me, still in his flying gear, chin-strap undone. I dared not look him in the face.

"You know I'm not allowed to carry heavy weights, Lord. How am I supposed to cope with this lot?" I remonstrated.

A quiet, slightly American voice beside me murmured, "Isn't that what I'm here for?" I looked down; it was Margaret speaking.

At that time, in my waking life, Margaret weighed not much more than five-and-a-half stone. She was in no way a fully committed Christian, close friend though she had become.

I hope that the wording was more respectful, but the gist of my next remark was, "That doesn't make sense, Lord. It's stupid!"

As I grew to realise much later, the Lord does not stop to argue. In no time at all, I was in the room with the picture window. The books had been carried in to the house and were arranged, spines uppermost, still in their baskets on the central table.

Flo, from the stone cottages opposite, was reaching across the books.

"*The Hiding Place*?" she noted. "I've heard of that. Who's read *The Hiding Place*?"

There was an embarrassed silence; the meringue-arranging ladies tittered and nudged each other at the sideboard, dissociating themselves from the others.

Then Margaret's quiet voice offered, "Do you see out of the window over there?... across the fields... there's a little roof-top peeping up. Mrs Smith lives there. She's read *The*

Hiding Place. If you put your boots on and go down the lane to her, she'll welcome you and tell you all about it. She'll have a good warm fire for you, too – and probably a cup of tea."

My heart warmed to the suggestion. Sharing books seemed such an informal, friendly way for Mrs Smith and Flo to get together and talk about things that mattered, regardless of denomination or even of any Christian commitment at all. Hazel and I had struggled to reach people like Flo and Mrs Smith in out-of-the-way places; often enough we had given as presents books from the Ark which might or might not meet an individual's need, and which in any case might only be of passing value. Here was a way to reach many more people with Christian books, people who might never reach the Ark; here was a way for Flo to taste and see, and to read without the need to lay out her own scarce cash; here was a way to go on feeding Mrs Smith with an ever-changing diet of fresh books.

My dreams were not all as coherent as this one obviously was. Dreams usually fade on waking, but I found during the next few days that this one would not go away.

As soon as I arrived back in the Ark to do my half-day's work, I hurried into the office to tell it all to Hazel. She was busy adding figures and was not to be interrupted. It was my job to comb the newly arrived catalogues in order to select fresh publications for sale in the shop, but I could not settle to this until I had told my dream. It was almost like being the bearer of tremendously exciting news.

Eventually Hazel finished totting up her column. "Can I tell my news? It's about a dream I had. There was a little van..."

"Yes?" Hazel sat back from her additions. "If it's not important at the moment, I don't want to know."

"It *is* important. It's about a new way of serving other people – in a tiny van. Very unpretentious... a dear little white van..."

"We haven't got a little van – or a big one either now, thank God! You know I can't cope with running this place much longer, with or without you. It's all grown too big. You know we need to save for a paid, full-time manager. Talk of another van is plain ridiculous." She reached for the next invoice and settled back to her work.

I felt chastened. Her words were true. Trade in the Ark was slack at that time of year; yet we had never been "in the red" and in due course, provided we ceased giving away our surplus funds in gifts of books, we should be able to save enough to employ a manager. But there was absolutely no hope of the Ark being in a position to buy or stock a van, let alone maintain it. The thought of there being no predictable income from a library service did indeed sound ridiculous. Mortified at my own dizzy dreams, I too settled down to work.

At the time I was grieved that there did not seem any way in which the little van could be dove-tailed in with the Ark. Only later did I come to see that the library work needed to stand on its own.

I still felt that the dream had to be told. The more I suppressed it the more it sizzled around inside me, as if I were a pressure cooker ready to burst. So I told my praying friends, and others, living and working in the countryside, people who were not accustomed to shop or to forgather in the Ark. The response was positive: each confirmed in one way or another that this was right.

During the next few months, in a mysterious way, God himself confirmed it. The dream presented such an attractive idea that I had been worried lest I should set out on a venture that was not according to his will. So I made no attempt to finance the project or to ask for funds. We as a family could not maintain our own rusty car, let alone buy a van. Yet people were led to send or offer small, tangible gifts: five pounds from one source, a Victorian night-gown, a Christening veil dating from the beginning of this century, a large volume of antique prints, ten pounds from another source, a silver-plated teapot, even an electric fire given by a blind lady. We sold the gifts and I put all the money away in a building society account, to await developments. There were also letters of encouragement, one from the Mother Abbess of a convent many miles away, another from Eric Abbott, the retired Dean of Westminster. Clergy from country parishes near and far were commenting upon the way their people could benefit from the proposed service. Slowly I began to realise that the network of those praying spread right across England.

Meanwhile Margaret had been encouraging me to grow stronger after my hysterectomy by persuading me to go on long dog-walks with her. I told her about the van dream, but was wary of mentioning her part in it. I knew she was not interested in Christian activities and was looking for a salaried post. I instinctively knew too that I should not invite anyone to have anything to do with the library service. They had to receive a definite indication themselves, independently of me. However, when I told her of the dream her immediate wistful comment was,

"I'm sure I'm involved in that somewhere, aren't I?"

It was difficult to know how to answer and so I slid round the question. Margaret was still battling with her anorexia. It was making her so weak that she could hardly turn the steering wheel of her car. She looked terribly ill and was worried because she needed to pass her British driving test before her American licence expired. Having failed one, she had negotiated with the examiners to retake her test in Lincoln. These matters were of vital importance to her in relation to any future job. Talk of library vans seemed irrelevant.

Instead we drove, in a different car, with a lighter steering system, all over the countryside. We practised in Lincoln. Then the day of the test arrived. Once I had left her at the testing station I hurried off to explore on foot all the alleyways around the cathedral. As I wandered from second-hand bookshop to fashion boutique, I suddenly realised that I should be praying for Margaret.

"Lord, is it fair to ask that she should pass?"

Silence.

"Well, Lord, she's my friend. She's had such a load of

trouble in the past few years that it's small wonder she's anorexic. I know you love her. If she's safe on the roads, then, please, make her pass!"

Suddenly I knew that all was well. Margaret was going to be driving me home in triumph. I also knew that I had to tell her why it was she had passed. That could be very embarrassing. We did not easily talk about prayer.

Margaret emerged from examination totally mystified. "I can't understand it. I made not one of my usual mistakes. I even answered all the questions easily and correctly. There was no way in which he could fail me, even if he'd wanted to. But he was a nice examiner. It's fantastic!"

Once I had rejoiced with her, I falteringly confessed that I had prayed for her.

"I'm not in the least surprised," she laughed. "There's no way in which I could have done that test, naturally speaking. My reflexes are far too slow and feeble at the moment." She proceeded to demonstrate that fact on her way home, but now it no longer mattered. Small escapades onto the grass verge and involving no other traffic became cause for relieved hilarity. It was the beginning, too, of indications for Margaret that God really did treasure her.

Life began to take on new dimensions for both of us now. I was learning all there was to know about photography, because Margaret was a keen, skilled photographer. I wanted to share her interest in this and so bought an intricate, fairly expensive camera and spent many hours standing around in the dark room of a photographic warehouse. The chemical smells and the dark seemed somehow to typify the sombre, reclusive life Margaret had been leading.

She, for her part, was becoming more involved with my work through the Ark. She offered her car and her driving skills for the use of a family visiting their son in prison. This could have been particularly gruelling for her, because her most recent connection with prisons and prisoners had been at the time of her daughter's death. Waiting with our visiting orders, in a room with those who had come to see a member of their closest family, was a moving experience. I felt like an intruder, in a situation where emotions were jangling: frustration, resentment, hatred, yearning, or sheer bitterness. I longed to communicate something of Jesus' compassion. That was possible only with the family of the lad we were there to visit. It was through him that we learned that one of our books had been read by his cell-mate, who had as a result come to know Jesus as Lord.

It was during this gruelling time of discussing and sharing the needs of these people that I came to have deeper conversations with Margaret. We searched through areas of our own encounters with God until we found places where we felt and understood alike. But every time the matter came up of commitment to Christ, as Lord of our daily living, Margaret skirted around the conversation. She declared very firmly that she was not yet ready.

Together we trudged on innumerable dog-walks across the summer countryside. There were times when her new puppy would not behave, trying instead to chase the swallows across the sky, causing me much mirth – but, to my disconcertment, distressing Margaret.

"If I cannot even control my own dog, what can I do?" she wept.

Gradually I realised that God's jewel had accumulated so much mud from the world's ill use that she could not value herself at all. Yet I knew how much I genuinely valued her; and that was only a shadow of the great self-giving love Jesus had waiting for her, when she was ready to receive it.

There came a time as we walked across acres of stubble field that I was unexpectedly given another picture. This time I was among a "harvest home" procession of workers: men, women and children carrying sheaves of corn, romping along, singing on their way, always moving onwards. They were tossing messages and snatches of song in laughter, one to another. Margaret, by contrast, was sitting on a barbed wire fence, the barbs firmly lodged in her backside, not only unwilling, but almost unable to jump off.

While I was witnessing this scene in my mind's eye,

Margaret had walked on ahead. I watched her lone figure striding on and realised that spiritually the choice before her had suddenly become urgent. The agony on her face as she had sat on that barbed wire fence was evidence of her longing to rollick along with God's family in the harvest home.

I had been a part of that procession. I did not want to leave her: yet somehow my staying back with her was delaying us both. My old friends, who had in times past cheered, supported, strengthened me were beckoning us both onward and neither of us wanted to miss their joy. They were obeying their Lord and I was dithering around, failing him both if I went ahead without Margaret and if I stayed behind while she perched on those barbs. She had to decide to get down and join us all; the Lord would show her how; I knew I could not.

Meanwhile her slender figure had stalked further off, but she turned and waited. I realised that I was by now sitting disconsolately on a bank, a sorry sight that needed some sort of explanation. So I got up, joined her and described that barbed wire fence. Nothing more was said.

Days after that, while walking in September woodland, Margaret and I prayed. After a struggle, she received her Lord afresh; her self-deprecation left her; she no longer hated herself or her body; she started to eat nutritious food, even cow's milk to which she had become allergic. Around that time I told her of the part she played in the dream about the van. The new life and light of Jesus shone from her in sheer joy.

It was now autumn. At the Ark, the Trustees had selected and appointed John as our first salaried manager. He was a member of the original management committee. As a full-time librarian he had been generous in giving his spare time, originally in sorting out the second-hand books and later as organiser of the records and tapes selection of the Ark's display. Now he had resigned from his secure post with the county library and undertaken to live on a reduced salary.

The vision for the mini-van had happened in the spring. Money had continued to arrive, including an anonymous

gift of five hundred pounds. The sum accumulated in the
building society was in the region of seven hundred and
seventy-five pounds.

On a Friday morning at the end of October, I was sitting
up in bed having a time of prayer when I heard the welcome
plop of the local paper on the doormat. In no time I was
clambering back into bed, armed with the week's gossip,
oblivious of the Lord. It was only when I saw a photograph
of John, inside the back page, alongside the caption, *Ark
appoints Manager*, that I realised that I and God, in that
order, had been having a conversation!

"I'm sorry, Lord. Did you want to say something more?"

Into my head came the whisper, "Van!"

"Yes. You keep reminding me, but what can I do? I don't
even know how much a little white van would cost."

Immediately I knew. There in front of me was the
Miscellaneous Sales section of the local paper.

"But I've looked in there from time to time over the year
and there hasn't been a little white van."

"Look now."

There were three vans altogether, and all priced below the
seven hundred and seventy-five pounds we had been given.

"But how can I tell whether a van is any good?"

"Haven't we gone through that one before, when I sent the
Ark library van to your back lane?"

It was half-term. All the children and Hugh were at home.
I did not want to go and see vans. Besides, I had my day's
programme already filled: my hair was to be cut and
shampooed in the morning; in the afternoon I must do my
work in the Ark office. As a gesture, I telephoned Margaret,
to inform her of the three white vans in the local newspaper.

On arrival at the hairdresser's I was told that Margaret
would be collecting me as soon as my hair was cut, "to see a
van, or something?"

"She jolly well won't. I have to shampoo my hair as soon
as I'm home."

Returned home, my head in an upstairs wash-basin, I
heard my elder daughter, Juliet, shouting, "Mum!" How

much longer are you going to be? Margaret's standing here in the hall, waiting for you!"

So it was that I was dragged by the wet forelock to look at vans. Margaret had already discounted one. It was in a shed in a nearby village, would have to be dragged out by tractor into the farmyard for inspection, had a permanent puddle on the driver's floor and had only one door at the back. The other two were at a Service Station, which augured well for a book service. One was very evidently covered in rust. The other looked good. Its number plate was XLU – Christ loves you.

"We'll bring a mechanic to see it tomorrow, if we may," I volunteered. Margaret offered to put down what I understood to be a deposit.

"O.K., me duck. See you tomorrow. God bless!"

As we walked away, my ears pricked up. "God bless!, he said! Let's have it. Let's put down the full payment now."

"But I have!" blurted Margaret apologetically.

14. No Going Back!

Now was the time for the Devil's minions to come in on the attack. The first feeling I had after Margaret's admission was one of panic: I had assumed that the Lord would prepare the ground very carefully for the purchase of a van, but the choice and decision had been made within half a morning. Close on the heels of panic came doubt: I was not convinced that this was necessarily the right van, even less that anything was to be achieved by buying it. After that followed fear: I was responsible, with Margaret, for whatever went wrong while we were driving it and since I now had no independent income the financial implications were enormous. With a rueful chuckle to cover all this, I jumped into Margaret's passenger seat and returned to the security of the family fold, and lunch. I was so appalled at what we had done that I had no heart to tell anyone until I had grown used to the fact.

However, within hours, I was to enjoy some reassurance. Nan, the elderly blind lady who had given us an electric fire to sell, months before, now came regularly to the Ark coffee bar to hear the news and for fellowship. She heard that I had arrived for my afternoon duties, and demanded that I come and sit beside her. I was in no mood to pass the time of day, but I obeyed. Richard, Stella's husband, was making Nan some coffee.

"Ros, my dear, there's something rather special I want to ask you." Nan took my hand and leaned confidentially towards me. "Do you remember in the spring mentioning a little white van in a dream?"

"Yes, Nan. I think I do," I muttered dismissively.

"Well, the silliest thing happened to me last night. I was in the driver's seat of that little van. It was a dream . . . We were on the edge of some woodland . . . very beautiful, dark trees . . . and the windscreen – now, don't you laugh," she chuckled, " – the windscreen had 'Ros' wirtten on it. Now how I was supposed to drive with that on it, I have no idea. But of course I can't drive because I'm blind. I'm going to be involved in all that somehow."

Richard had overheard. "Talking of vans, Ros. When are you getting that van you told us about in the spring? I said to the Lord last night, I said, 'Lord, I've been asking you to give her that van on and on, but you don't do anything. Now come on, Lord, or I'll give up asking!' so when are you getting it, Ros?"

"We'll have to see. Thanks for praying, Richard."

I disengaged my hand from Nan's. She grasped it again more firmly. "You don't think I'm silly, do you?"

"No. Thanks for telling me. I'll talk about it all more, soon. But right now, I've got loads to do in the office." I hurried upstairs, baffled, delighted and silent.

Next day, our local mechanic diagnosed two or three small matters that needed to be put right with the van, including a new gearbox. So we must wait till the following Thursday finally to collect it.

Meanwhile John's service of dedication as the new manager took place and he was in the office on duty on the Monday afternoon when I arrived. The plan now was for Hazel and me to continue unofficially as support for John as long as he wanted our help. As soon as I arrived I was filled with delight and joy to see him and gave him a big congratulatory hug. Having had the weekend to collect my thoughts about the van, I was ready and glad to tell John that it was in our possession, and nearly ready for use. His first reaction was one of delight.

Later in the afternoon, and in the ensuing weeks, John was noticeably less enthusiastic about the van. At a subsequent meeting of the Ark Trustees, it was to be made abundantly clear to me that the Ark could not be associated with it. The need to pay a full-time manager preoccupied the minds of at least some of the Trustees: a free library service could not be seen as contributing to sales in the bookshop.

I was puzzled and a little hurt. Why ever was this van being so roundly disowned? Was the buying of it in some way a threat to us at the Ark? Would a library service take away sales from the shop? Was I very wrong to have bought the van at all?

I tried hard to answer the questions as an Ark Trustee. It was something we had not been able to afford, but here it was, offered to us on a plate. I thought of the local library, standing on the same street in the town as the main bookshop. If I found a book I enjoyed in the library, I would buy it at the shop. I might pick up a book in the shop and want to read it before deciding to pay for it. If I had read a library copy, I might buy several copies as presents for others. On the other hand I might not. It was all very confusing. As I prayed about it I saw again the library standing serenely in the High Street, complementing the book shop. Somehow, all felt well.

Next morning, Margaret and I prayed long and hard about the whole project. We had many confirmations that the van ministry was right, but we continued to be puzzled about the response of people at the Ark. All we could do, according to the Scriptures we had been reading, was to "let love abound," until we could understand more. Then we had to think whatever to call the little van.

"Father, you know I'm no use whatsoever at thinking up gimmicky names. It was Derek who thought of the Ark's name. That was clever. But whatever do we call a van?"

I toyed with a few ideas but got nowhere at all. The man who had sold us the van had commented that these were often used as news vans... Glumly I opened my eyes. The first thing I saw was my Bible; the title embossed on the cover was *Good News Bible*.

News van

Good – news van

Good News Van.

There was the answer. Margaret grinned her approval.

Then together we discussed what colour would be appropriate for the white van's lettering. Blue came vividly to mind, as we talked. Blue writing on a white background was what was used on the Anglian Water Authority's vans. There had been one or two comments about how the Christian library would bring springs of living water to a dry land. Now here was a link that made sense.

That afternoon a young curate from a nearby market town came into the shop and up to the office for a chat.

"Michael, we've got the little van you thought was such a good idea."

"Wonderful! Where are you going to start?"

"That's our problem. We've no idea how to begin. We know we're supposed to use the sending out of the seventy disciples by Jesus as our model, and so we should be welcome where we go. The 'peace should be returned' to us. Any suggestions?"

"Why don't you try Tony Gough, the vicar of Lyddington? He's very good news for Rutland, I think."

"Good news!" Had I mentioned the new name? I searched my memory and realised that Michael did not yet know the lettering to be written on the van. So here was confirmation, and also a potential launching pad at Lyddington. I felt a great peace welling over me.

That afternoon the Collins representative called in the office. Before John and he settled to their first business together the rep. paused.

"Let me first wish you both the early compliments of the season!" He handed each of us a tiny diary. It was a Good News Diary. Idly I thumbed my way through to the illustrated text opposite my birthday week. The wording was, "Perfect love casts out fear." This was precisely the Fatherly reassurance I needed, first for the van's name and secondly with how to handle personal hiccups in its early encounters.

I telephoned Tony Gough, who responded warmly to the whole concept of the Good News ministry. He fixed an appointment for us to drive it on its maiden trip from the service station, straight to his vicarage in the heart of Rutland.

Margaret and I collected the van from the service station. As I settled into the low driver's seat and eyed the enormous lorries roaring past me I was once again assailed by fear. However, I could see Margaret's comforting Fiesta in the rear mirror and felt protected. We left her car in Stamford and drove straight on to Lyddington. As we reached the crest of a lane beside one red ploughed hill, and surveyed the great wide valley below us, its grey stone villages nestling in comfortable hollows, I realised that this was to be our place of work, our promised land.

However, the van was behaving in a far less romantic way. Its new gearbox was like an arthritic knee-joint in an elderly lady. There was no way in which it could be persuaded to change into reverse. We arrived in Lyddington, to our great satisfaction after several wrong turnings, and travelled along its main street, flanked with golden stone cottages. We decided that the church should be near the vicarage and so we studied all the cottages in that area carefully. However we found nothing and very soon realised that we had run out of houses or cottages to scan. The village had ended. Straight ahead of us stretched a long, straight lane. A herd of cattle were lumbering ruminatively towards us, pausing to consider us and moving slowly past on their way to milking ... and I had to turn a van which refused to reverse. We were being introduced to the hazards of pastoral evangelism in a fairly immediate way. "In all things give thanks," I thought. The only solution was to drive straight ahead with joyful abandon to the Lord's providence and manoeuvre the van into a U-turn. I did this while the herdsman watched, with dropped jaw. Blessedly the lane's grass verges did not have cross-drains and I was soon back amongst the cows. I pushed the driver's window back.

"Can you direct me to the vicarage, please?"

"Vicarage? Easy! It's not labelled, of course, but it's the very first house you come to."

Tony was very helpful. He told us of several of his

parishioners who would be delighted to borrow some books and promised to tell them who we were before we introduced ourselves. As we left he came out to inspect the van and to bless it.

"The only difficulty is, it won't reverse!" I commented ruefully.

"Won't reverse? That's splendid news. That means there's no going back..."

The next time I saw Margaret she was quietly bubbling with excitement. We had accumulated several boxes of second-hand books and she had bought five bright red plastic baskets. Now she had been given one hundred pounds with which to buy a quantity of new Christian paperbacks. Soon we had "five baskets full".

Our next problem was the lettering of the van. Sign-writer's charges were far too costly. Then I thought of Richard, who had been so helpful with the renovation of the Ark building. The writing of his notices had been immaculate. Perhaps he would agree to be our sign-writer?

It was important that the van should go out on its first trips the following week in its new insignia; and so Richard agreed to come as soon as he was free, the following Saturday morning. However, as we came away from the Ark prayer meeting that morning, he told us that he would unfortunately not be able to come and write our sign, because his family was expecting visitors.

Panic and frustration assailed me.

"Lord, what are we supposed to do?"

My mind raced around all the friends I knew, wondering who was artistic, who would be free at such short notice, who would be even willing to undertake such a job. I drew a blank.

"Do it yourself."

"But Father, you know I'm no use at that sort of thing. I don't know what sort of paint to get. It would have to be permanent. Suppose it ran all down the white sides of our van... Besides, it's Saturday and the children are home from school."

"If it's worth doing, do it yourself."

"Of course it's worth doing. We can't go out in our own strength. We've got to proclaim that it's a Christian book service, bringing your Good News."

I was about to pass a paint shop, and so I parked my bicycle. After some deliberation and plenty of guidance from the assistant, I was cycling home with two shades of blue enamel paint and some brushes. The only lettering I felt at all happy about producing was the kind used by my children at playschool. I grabbed the nearest cardboard box and scrawled a great G on it. The two O's expressed my frustration: they were interlinked, cross-eyed. As I continued hacking out the thick cardboard the phone rang. It was Richard. His visitors' car had broken down. They were likely to be up to three hours late arriving. He could come and do any sign-writing we wanted.

"But I fail to see how I'm going to get 'Good News Van' on the little panel on the side of a mini in a script that is legible from a distance."

"I've already cut out some letters. They're big and will go on at any angle."

As Richard experimented with my crazy stencils he commented: "This is remarkable. The only way big letters like this will fit on is if they bounce up and down. What a good idea. Very cheering!"

Awed, I remembered the child-like atmosphere of the original dream. Even my panic, frustration and incompetence were being used to glorify God's work. I almost felt him chuckling at me...

We had now been given enough money to insure and stock the van and to retax it when the time came. To begin with we had five baskets full of lively Christian books and two invitations to visit, arranged by Tony Gough.

The first time I drove the newly painted white van into the back lane, I saw my retired doctor in gardening clothes, wheeling his wheelbarrow. I felt very conspicuous; I wished I was wearing some sort of disguise until we were well out of Stamford. Blessedly, Margaret did not share my embarrassment. She did not expect anyone to notice us. They did not!

We were shy, too, when we arrived at Janet's house in a Rutland village. Janet was a part-time nurse. She had not invited any friends to share the books over coffee, because she herself was unsure of us. However, once we had explained ourselves and our hopes for the van she was thrilled.

We unloaded our baskets of books from their stacks on two trolleys and let Janet browse freely. She was delighted to find copies of two or three books she had eyed on other people's shelves or in shops.

"Surely these can't be free? How many can I borrow?"

I thought quickly. "Do we let her have as many as she wants, Lord? You said, 'Freely give'. So, how many?"

The answer came inside me: "Think of your own library experience."

Aloud, I declared to Janet, "You may have any two: one to get bored with and one to enjoy, probably!" Then as an afterthought I added, "There are no strings attached. You won't be examined on what you've read when we come again." Janet looked incredulous.

"However do you make ends meet? Isn't there some sort of fee or subscription? Or are you doing it so as to persuade me to join some organisation?"

Margaret explained that we had no other motive than to lend her the kind of Christian books we enjoyed reading, that we asked for no payment and that Jesus in His own good time prodded those who were to give. We talked about the books with Janet and noted in a filing system what she chose, promising to return in a month's time for her to change her books.

We talked, too, about many interests we had in common. She soon became such a good friend that we began to wonder whether we could really call this work ... Sitting in the corner of her sitting-room, rocking to and fro in a play-pen, was her youngest child, a dark-haired lad with some sort of disability that had slowed down his progress badly. He took no notice of us and very little of the stimulating,

brightly-coloured toys all around him. He just rocked
backwards and forwards, blowing bubbles to himself. We
enquired after all the children and were told that, although
his two elder sisters were alert and intelligent, some damage
had happened to Harry at his birth. Janet assured us that
Harry had been prayed for, but that any further prayer of
ours on a continuing basis would help him. Over the course
of several return van visits we were to see Harry begin to take
notice, then stand up, walk, become himself. This was to be
the first of an increasing number of visits the little van was to
make. Janet began to tell her neighbours about our visits. In
no time she was holding monthly coffee parties for eight or
ten people to borrow our books.

The elderly lady who had given us the original hundred
pounds for new stock was observing our progress closely.
She approached Margaret again, this time with some
indignation.

"Do you mean to say that's all you can get for one hundred
pounds? Well, I think I'm supposed to give you a bit more.
I'd expected you to buy twice as much. You'd better have a
further hundred!"

A visit to a rambling farmhouse in another village gave us
yet more encouragement.

"It's good to meet more Christians we can pray with! We
have read many of these books, but we're discovering lots
more we've not been able to afford yet. Here, have this stack
from our own shelves. These will boost your supplies. We'll
invite the neighbours in next time. They could be interested."

We rattled our way from the farm to the top of the hill, the
tang of goat cheese and watercress sandwiches still lingering,
glad to be at work, glad to be alive!

In December a team of Christians arrived in town, eager
to explore the possibilities of some sort of evangelistic
outreach. At the last minute, two of the leaders of the team
were billeted with us. I was disconcerted and delighted all at
once: delighted, because I had met the two we were to receive
before and found what they were doing invigorating and
encouraging; disconcerted because I had no clear informa-

tion about the nature of their visit. Besides, our family diary for that weekend was full and the house a tip.

There was just enough time for me to sort out the last problem. I rushed around the house with a vacuum cleaner and duster, made up the guest beds and put a vase of flowers on the dressing table just as the front door bell rang. Michael and Jane were a little cool in their greeting; I decided they must be weary from their journey. Michael had a pink and swollen nose, which he attributed, to my mortification, to dust allergy. They quickly disappeared to their room, without any exchange of news. After a hasty evening meal they were gone, to join the rest of their team and to plan their schedule.

They left me feeling vaguely uncomfortable. There had not been any of the friendliness and openness which I had expected with them. Why were they so distant with Hugh and the children? Was there something wrong? Was Michael feeling unwell? Could they not remember meeting us before?

I was eager to exchange news with them and especially to tell them all about the Good News Van. Next morning, Michael and Jane were sitting in the kitchen long before I came down to prepare breakfast for them. Our family was still fast asleep, except for Hugh, who had to be in school first thing. Now seemed an opportune moment. We started to chat, and I was soon pouring out the story of the van, at first in great joy; but I admitted my bewilderment and sadness at the response of some of the Ark Trustees.

"I'd do anything to clear the air and make sure everyone was friends again. Well... almost anything," I corrected.

Michael and Jane looked solemn. Michael cleared his throat. "Can we move to somewhere more private than this kitchen? After all, the children will be buzzing around here soon."

In silence we adjourned to the sitting-room. It was then that it became apparent that they had already been influenced by the opposition.

"For the sake of the unity of the brethren, would you be prepared to give up the Good News Van?"

The Scriptural wording was persuasive. "Give it up?" I asked inside myself. "Lord, what do *you* want me to do? Is that the answer? Shall I just give it up?"

My head felt an immediate and tremendous pressure from a Presence above me, in me, surrounding me, commanding,

"Go into all the world and preach the Gospel!"

There was no questioning that order. I heard my own voice, very small and distant, utter one word, in answer to Michael and Jane.

"No."

15. Tiny Battalions

During the summer, before the van became a reality, Hugh and I and the children had attended The Christian Families Conference, under canvas at Canterbury. Towards the end of the week, Dennis Ball spoke at the evening praise meeting. I settled in my seat, just in front of Richard, the engineer from Stamford, one trustee who was particularly supportive of the van idea. The conference had been heartening, but the week was drawing to a close and Richard's presence behind me reminded me of the constraint and doubt I had sensed while in Stamford.

Dennis moved forward into the arc-lights on the platform, but announced that he was about to put on his "other hat" prior to addressing the conference on that evening's theme. He began to question us:

"I don't know how many of you live near open countryside, but thousands of acres of Great Britain consist of that. There is of course the odd village or two and many isolated farm-houses. My concern is for the people who live in these remote rural areas. Some of them are fully committed Christians; they have little or no opportunity for fellowship, apart from that provided from time to time in the parish church or in the chapel. Many thousands more have only a vague idea who Jesus Christ was, having heard about him, when they listened, in school and having forgotten him as part of their childhood. Some hear a little more if they have television. Most are so busy working among the beasts or out on the land that the very suggestion of church is ridiculous pie-in-the-sky. They have little idea of the whereabouts of the nearest practising Christian and assume that it is the vicar's job to look after all that sort of thing, he being the only one who has time or inclination. *These people are starved*."

A sharp tingle ran down my spine and legs, making me feel as if I had been struck by lightning. Dennis seemed to be talking directly to me. Yet he was going on to talk of his involvement with a movement called Rural Evangelism, Mission for Christ. He described much of their work, but made no mention of any kind of Christian travelling library. I turned to Richard and Josephine, and noted the light of encouragement in their eyes. It was several weeks before Hugh pointed out the address in an advertisement in *Buzz* magazine. In answer to my enquiries, the secretary at Mission for Christ sent me all the publicity, including the most recent newsletter. On the back of that was a photograph of the open rear of a vehicle full of books. The caption explained that these were being sold from village to village in the Scottish Border country. I wrote again, asking Mission for Christ whether they had ever conceived the idea of a travelling library; the answer was negative, but there was plenty of encouragement for us to go ahead with our "exciting work" and an invitation to apply to become affiliated to Mission for Christ with the status of Christian Workers.

Margaret and I were disappointed. We felt very new and raw and had been searching for some precedent, for someone somewhere who had the wisdom of experience with which to advise us on the pitfalls and joys of running a free Christian travelling library. But we sent off our references and duly became Accredited Christian Workers for Mission for Christ. It was reassuring to know that we had some "umbrella" group who would be praying for us. Later, when we were asked by the suspicious under what authority we worked, it was astonishing how acceptable people found our standing with Mission for Christ. When the Christian Book Service grew more extended, we were to need not only their prayer and encouragement but also their guidance with the charitable gifts we received.

We did have prayer backing more immediately at Stamford. One of the outcomes of going to the Families Conference in Canterbury was the need for those of us who went to continue living in the new life of the Holy Spirit. For me this was a rich and extraordinary experience which could not easily be accepted by the congregation where I worshipped. In fact there were many who were antipathetic to the suggestion that the gifts of the Holy Spirit were available to the Church in the 1970s; the whole subject was distasteful and smacked of enthusiasm, as I myself well knew from my previous existence. The friends who had been at Canterbury and who came from other churches in Stamford were meeting the same bleak response. Yet each of us knew we should stay within the framework of an established denomination. So we agreed to meet together at the one time when our churches and the other societies of the town were almost certain not to have a regular gathering. Our aim was to rejoice together in the Lord, to learn from him, to pray and to minister to one another, generally to encourage and sustain each other in loving fellowship.

When Tony Gough, the vicar of Lyddington, heard about this, he asked Margaret and me to bring our Sunday evening "Canterbury" group over to Stoke Dry, one of his parishes. He invited the Christians in his area to meet together at the Old Manor there, for an evening of fellowship. We were doubtful about how this would work out among people who hardly knew each other. However, it was Christmas time and it struck me how so very often we forget the Royal Person whose birthday it is just as soon as we have unwrapped our own presents and fed ourselves into oblivion. So, during Christmas week itself, about fourteen of our own fellowship piled into a car and a minibus, guitar and tambourine at the ready, and asked the Lord to bless the evening. To our delight, Tony had brought together another fourteen, including young children; several of them had musical instruments at the ready and everyone was eager to learn what happened next. At our informal gatherings in Stamford, no one in particular had been in the lead. We were

met to worship and listen to the Lord, and we relaxed as he
led us in his ways. Now, however, there were not just one, but
two or three clergy present. I wondered whatever would
happen. The coffee-drinking and the friendly chatter went
on long enough for me to begin to hope that perhaps that
was all that was required on this particular evening.
However, the noise suddenly subsided and everyone looked
expectantly towards me. I in turn looked expectantly
towards Tony Gough. He took a lively interest in the dog
and waited. Someone twanged a guitar in a desultory way. In
a small voice I asked what tune the guitarist was trying to
play. Quite suddenly we were all singing away as if we were a
group of songsters accustomed to break out in harmony with
each other over the old favourites. Just as suddenly the
singing came to an end.

"Someone usually has a Scripture reading that they want
to share with the rest of us now... Has anyone anything
special?"

There was an awkward silence. I prayed inwardly, trying
hard to trust the Lord to show someone what he wanted.
One or two of the older men shifted uncomfortably in their
seats. A woman looked at her watch. The children wriggled
against each other. Then Lucy, a girl of about nine, offered:

"I've got a favourite verse" My heart sank. One favourite
verse? How could we make an evening's discussion out of
that? Or rather, however would the Lord?

"Father, help!" I breathed inwardly.

"Come on, then, Lucy. What is it?" asked her mother.

Lucy read out one simple verse of thanksgiving from her
favourite psalm: "Praise the Lord, O my soul, and forget not
all his benefits." As soon as she had explained briefly why
she delighted in it, her theme was taken up eagerly by various
people across the room. It was like playing "Pass the Parcel"
with a package of praise. Each one had some experience to
relate of how the Lord had been revealing his presence at the
heart of life here and now.

Gradually we began to realise that there were also matters
for intercession, even prayer for healing. The younger

children crept off to bed; there were more songs and more thanksgivings; eventually Hugh, observing the teenagers installed on the broad manor-house window-sill, submitted his contribution from the Scriptures:

"Many lamps were burning in the upstairs room where we were meeting. A young man named Eutychus was sitting in the window, and as Paul kept on talking, Eutychus got sleepier and sleepier, until he finally went sound asleep and fell from the third storey to the ground..." (Acts 20:8,9)

Tony suggested that this kind of fellowship should be made available to anyone in the surrounding countryside whom we visited with the Good News Van. He suggested hiring the village hall in Lyddington, Rutland, for the first public Good News Fellowship, this time to celebrate our Risen Lord, at Easter. When Tony suggested this, we were in the habit of visiting about five homes. I asked how many the hall seated.

"Oh, about ninety," was the reply.

"But we can't fill a hall that size!" I remonstrated.

"I thought the Lord did that sort of thing for us..." offered Tony. "Let's pray in around seventy, shall we? Good scriptural figure, you know."

I gulped, but said nothing. As we travelled around the countryside, lending our books, Margaret and I mentioned the Easter Good News Fellowship. "It will start around seven in the evening..."

"Oh, but I can't come till I've put the children to bed. My husband and I can't get anywhere till eight o'clock."

"That's right. Mine likes to eat, too, before he comes out."

"Don't worry," I reassured. "If we all bring a contribution that others can enjoy, your husband will be well fed."

Then, from a different household: "Isn't it starting till seven? Oh dear. The kids will be ravenous, but they're determined to come along. Of course, we'll have to leave soon after eight."

We began to realise that the Lord was going to have to design this get-together entirely his way. "The timing will be flexible," I declared firmly, "but those who want to eat had better be there by seven, sharp!"

Sadly, the number of those upon whom we had depended for support was dwindling rapidly.

"Easter? Why ever choose then? That's when the relations will be around."

"Bring them, too."

"It's not their sort of thing... At least, I suppose I could try. We'll see."

The morning of the Lyddington Fellowship came. Hugh had entered it in our family diary as "The Lyddington Seventy".

Beth, Tony Gough's wife, telephoned. "Can you give me a rough estimate of how many you expect to come this evening?"

"I've no idea," I apologised. "The one's who've said they'll try to come I can count on the fingers of one... no... perhaps two hands. Those who will definitely come: five of our family and you both, I suppose."

"Oh, there are several more in the village who will be helping. So you've no idea? It's a good thing it's only drinks we have to provide. Well, we'll go on praying."

Margaret and I drove the Good News Van along the main village street in the gloaming, wondering just what our heavenly Father was going to do. The lights were on in the village hall. The first thing that met my eye as I swung open the door was a row of trestle tables, the length of the room. And they were laden with food. I was carrying a big tray of potatoes in their jackets, still hot from our oven. I realised with dismay that we had forgotten the family margarine tub. But lined down the length of the table there were dishes of golden butter. The choice of food was worthy of a banquet: a choice of mushroom, bacon, spinach, chicken, or cheese quiches; cornish pasties; sausage rolls or just sausages on sticks; coleslaw, tossed green salad, tomatoes, celery; appetising rice dishes; meringues, jellies, trifles, bowls of fresh fruit; tea, coffee, cold drinks – even plain biscuits for those who had over-eaten! The Lord had provided abundantly through his people.

I looked up, wondering just who this milling throng were,
each of whom had contributed to this feast. There were
several of those whom we visited, after all, and they had told
their friends, had brought along their visiting relations, and
now were smiling in glad anticipation of a wonderful
evening. Best of all were the shy, welcoming grins of the men
we now knew well from the local Langley House trust home
for ex-offenders. At first they were of their own choice sitting
well apart, but it was not long before they were joined by
others and were singing songs of fellowship to the
accompaniment of guitar, piano, flute, tambourine – and
even a banjo. By the end of the evening, several of those who
had stayed on were asking for prayer for healing, were
seeking personal counselling and were going away rejoicing.

"How many were there here, tonight, Tony?" I asked as
the last sodden tea-towel was packed away. "Were there
nearly seventy after all?"

"As a matter of fact I counted ninety," twinkled Tony
casually.

It was not until the following summer, when one or two
more of these gatherings had met in neighbouring villages
that I felt a very strong urge to tell other Christians what the
Lord was doing. The dream of the Good News Van could be
used in other parts of Britain equally well. Our family went
to the Canterbury Christian Families conference again, this
time with Margaret and our blind friend, Nan. I searched for
Dennis Ball, in the hope of telling him what was now
happening with our little version of rural evangelism.
However, he was not at the conference. The Lord seemed to
be highlighting for me the compassionate and spontaneous
personality of Jean Darnall. Margaret and I made an
appointment to see her. We had to queue for what seemed
hours in the rain, outside her private caravan at the
conference ground. When eventually it was our turn to be
admitted, we hastily told the story of the van. I listened to
myself in dismay. Compared with what was happening in
Jean's ministry each evening in the big marquee, the
development of the Good News Fellowships seemed

pathetic. I faltered to a standstill.

"I don't really know why we had to tell you all that."

Jean's face glowed. "It's just wonderful!" she purred. "As you were talking, I could see the Lord gathering together tiny battalions of his heavenly army, dotted right across the nation. Each little group is polishing up its heavenly armour in preparation for the end-times battle ... Now, before you go again, let me just pray for you two dear girls."

We were already standing and so Jean had to reach up in order to lay hands on our heads. When she had finished asking the Lord to bless us, to guide us, to endue us with his love, trust, obedience and wisdom, she stood back.

"I just had another glorious picture. It was of you two at God's heavenly banquet ... Not seated, mind ... No, you're just servants ... but you're carrying enormous trays, laden with food for God's own dear people, fruit that most of them have never tasted before. Now isn't that just great?"

16. Behind Locked Doors

The December night was drawing in early at the Ark. I had had a busy afternoon and was now checking the till, before locking up and hurrying home to feed the children. Christmas and Christmas cards had been the constant theme of the bookshop conversations. Colin was still lurking in the coffee bar, alone.

"Aren't you going home, Colin? I'm locking up."

"Nowhere t'go." Colin's dark eyebrows were knit in misery.

"I thought you lived in Easton?"

"Mum and Dad do – and Chris. But not me no more."

"Why ever not?"

"Don't like what I get up to. Never have. Don't belong there, I don't."

Silence.

"What *do* you get up to?"

Silence. Colin patted each denim pocket in turn in a hunt for his cigarettes. Then he abandoned the search.

"Got anywhere I can stay? Like ... for Christmas?"

I realised that Colin knew that our house had a spare guest room. Yet Colin's parents would be very hurt if he chose to live away over Christmas. Besides, our own relations needed to be accommodated over that period.

"Why ever don't you go home, Colin?"

"Don't want to. They hate my guts."

I searched my mind among the different possibilities, but always Colin's home was the answer. I told him as much.

Colin hunched off into the night, groping again for his

cigarettes. I locked up the now empty shop and hurried home, chilled.

Two days later, when I was again in the Ark office, there was a telephone call from Grantham Police Station.

"Mrs Allan? We're holding in custody a young man here, name of Thompson. Is he known to you?"

"Yes."

"He has permission to have a brief conversation. I'll hand him to you."

"Are you going to come and see me, then?"

"What have you been up to?"

"Snatched a bag, didn't I? – on Monday evening. Didn't keep nothing. Need to see someone, though... Hang on... the copper's saying sommat... He says only relations and girl-friends... Yeah! You're my girl-friend ain't you?" He laughed. "Even if you do work in the week, you've got Sundays. You've got time. C'mon. I need to talk."

The following Sunday, Hugh drove me and the children on a family outing to the quiet market town of Grantham. I followed a policewoman who locked and unlocked doors, eventually locking me in with Colin, who, as usual, had little to say for himself. I had brought a comic-strip version of David Wilkinson's *The Cross and the Switchblade* for Colin to look at while held in custody.

"What happens next?"

"Lincoln? Dunno..." He shrugged.

At first Colin pleaded "not guilty" at the Magistrates' Court in Stamford, in the hope that he might remain free for a longer period. However, he was remanded in custody in Lincoln Jail until the Crown court hearing.

It was a strange experience, driving with Margaret up the familiar "driving test" hill towards the regal cathedral and then deviating away from familiar ground out on a bleak straight road to Her Majesty's Prison. As we neared the great gates and I thumped the polished brass door knocker I felt awed by the whole machinery of justice; at the same time I was at ease, deep down, with the awareness that the Prison Officer who slid aside the door-bolts was genuinely concerned that visitors to the prison should be reassured and at ease. I looked hard into his eyes, to see whether there was any of the compassion of Jesus. The tall archway, enclosed by a second pair of wrought-iron gates, resounded with sharp orders and the cold jangle of keys.

"Visitors to wait in here, please. Be ready to present visiting orders and to state the prisoner's number."

There was a notice, warning us all that we could give the prisoners no presents, that we could not proceed beyond the archway with a tape-recorder, radio or camera and that we were there entirely at the discretion of the prison authorities. I looked down at the heavy bag of new Christian paperbacks I had brought for Colin and his companions.

"Is it possible to speak to the Chaplain, please?" I asked at the window of the office facing the room I should have been in.

"No, duck. He's off duty. What d'you want?" It was the same officer who had let us in originally.

"Well, I have here some books I wanted to give him so that he could let the person I'm visiting see them."

"Is he expecting these?" The officer had come out of his room and was looking suspiciously at my bag. "All books given to prisoners must be new paperbacks without any marking," he recited. "They shall be requisitioned by the Prison Library. No books may be received by hand but must be sent in through the Post Office."

"These books are new. Have a look, do. If I can't give them direct to the prisoner, then the Chaplain can have them as a present. I'll write him a note, giving him the prisoner's number, too. Will that do?"

The officer was staring in amazed approval at the contents of my carrier bag. His eyes were beginning to twinkle.

"They look a cheerful enough lot to me," he grinned.

"You see, we've come forty miles to see the prisoner. It seems a waste to spend money going out again to post this load from the nearest Post Office."

"We'll show these to the Chaplain. Put your note in and leave it all with me."

The queue of visitors was now being mustered to await the clatter of the padlocks on the inner wrought-iron gates. The wind crept under my skirt, down my neck and all around my knees, as I looked up at the cheerless building in front of me. The barred cell windows were mute.

Colin's mother had come with us. In order to cheer the occasion she had dyed her hair plum red and was wearing her highest heels. Now evidently excited at the prospect of meeting her son, she followed the prison officer eagerly. Another door was unlocked. This time we were ordered into a waiting room full of mothers, girl-friends and children. A pall of smoke hung from the ceiling. Each little group was a defensive unit, unwilling to exchange remarks with strangers.

"What *is* this place, Mum?" A small boy kicked himself into a more manageable position on his mother's lap.

"It's an institution," volunteered his grandmother.

"Does Dad like insti – insti's?"

"Not much." His mother lit another cigarette and patted her hair.

"Why doesn't he come home, then?"

The ensuing baleful silence was broken by an order, "Visitors for Jenkins, Smith, Blake, Thompson, McGillivray and Haymes this way please!" We processed, this time in nonchalant disarray, into the Visits Room.

Colin, in striped blue prison shirt and blue denims, grinned nervously across at us from an empty table.

"How's that for the fire brigade?" He stared appraisingly at his mother's hairdo.

"None of your cheek," she bridled delightedly, "or you won't get any baccy."

"You can't give me none, anyway." Gleefully he reached into his denims pocket and started to roll his own slim cigarette. "I just have to earn it these days, don't I?"

The news was slow. Colin hoped to work in the mail-bag sewing shop. Some prisoners were detailed to sew the blue uniforms each man was wearing; but men on remand must spend nearly all their time in their cells, waiting and hoping. I wondered which of the men scattered across the Visits Room would one day read the books I had brought; which ones would find their way to Jesus as had Jim, a few years before, in prison for arson and now working hard at the Ark.

If the Lord had begun to show me what life was like for men in prison, he had still to show me the processes of justice in a Crown Court. The day for the trial had arrived. I was required to be a witness. Margaret came with me, concerned for what would happen to Colin who quite evidently was guilty, despite his plea. The court assembled in a desultory way. Solicitors consulted with each other. We all waited. Suddenly a panel behind the bench opened. A voice proclaimed, "The court will rise" and a dapper little man in scarlet emerged through the panel. Rubbing his hands he acknowledged us all with a bob of his wig. The hearing was brief. I was asked to speak to Colin's good character, but the only comments I could submit were that he was friendly, returned the correct change when sent out to buy biscuits for the coffee bar and was helpful. I omitted the facts that the biscuits were for his own consumption and that the helpfulness was in decorating the Ark stair-well with gloss paint instead of distemper. The fact that Colin had snatched a handbag was enough to have him sentenced. The judge leaned anxiously over his desk.

"Young man, you have behaved selfishly. You showed no respect for the lady concerned. Although you did not keep the bag or its contents your offence is robbery. If I were to release you, your next offence would probably be even more serious. I cannot sentence you to less than eighteen months." He adjusted his spectacles with a sniff of disdain. "Send him down." I was awestruck to see that in Lincoln Crown Court the prisoner is literally sent downstairs, under the dock.

The next year was spent ferrying one or the other Thompson parent to see Colin. They refused to travel together, each convinced that the other was guilty of bringing up Colin badly. In fact as the months passed and Colin was sent to a prison more than two hours' drive away, we grew to know and care for each of them. When divorce was threatened, in the course of one particularly bleak picnic, we realised that we had been doing everything but pray. Each time, we took yet more Christian books into the prison, until one day Colin muttered,

"If my cell-mate, Bryan, writes to you, will you write back? He needs it. He's gone nutty like you. Says he's a Christian. Read *Lonely but Never Alone* or sommat. Turned him on, it has. He'll be in trouble with the rest of us if he don't shut up." Colin looked hurt and puzzled.

Bryan did change, enough for the prison authorities to promote him to a block where men had many more privileges. He kept up a lively correspondence with my husband, enough to establish him in his faith and make sure he had a church fellowship to link up with when he was released. However, Colin's parents' negative attitude towards one another seemed to be hardening. Each month there was more talk about interviews with a solicitor and Mrs Thompson's hunt for accommodation. Each month, Colin was counting the days until his release and his proposed return at last to his family!

During a lunch-time break on the journey yet again to the prison, this time in November, Margaret went for a brief walk, leaving me alone with Mr Thompson. He was not his usual gaunt self. In fact he looked singularly sparkling and attentive.

"How's Mrs Thompson?" I expected the usual spate of complaints and half switched my attention.

"Capital!"

"What did you say?"

Mr Thompson swelled his shoulders and patted his chest with both hands. "She's capital. Give me this new coat. Always a good sign. I give her one, too. Do it every time we make up. Trouble is, I've got too many coats. Can't throw any of 'em out. Huh!"

I was overjoyed. Neither Margaret nor I had found anything to say to husband or wife that we thought could heal the rift between them. But we had prayed. Now Mrs Thompson, grinning all over on her next prison visit, volunteered,

"I've given up trying to move. We're going to have to make a go of it, for Colin's sake – and for Chris's. Me and Mr T. have decided we're going to have a big Christmas party to celebrate Colin's coming out. Going to be a big do it is."

She was to be disappointed on that very visit. Colin was almost inaudible.

"Got done for another week. New Year's Eve, now... Done for fighting... Four of us in one cell... What d'you expect?... Weren't me. I was asleep, but they jumped on me bunk. Landed on top of me... Cell's only meant for two... Stupid, it is... See you New Year's Eve... Or I might join up with someone in Leicester... Got a job for me there... a gang who've been out of here couple of months say they can do with me..."

"Well, they're not going to," retaliated Margaret, "because we're fetching you home."

"What, at eight in the morning? That's when they let you out and I'm coming out as fast as I can... with me rail fare to Leicester."

"Don't you want to go home, after all?"

"Yes. But can't make it... Too far... Connections and all... New Year's Eve... Never get there."

So Margaret and I set our alarms very early indeed. The dawn, when it came, emerged greyly through freezing fog. We were glad of its light after the confusing reflection of headlamps earlier, while it was still dark. A big hold-up was to reveal a tangle of lorry and car. The day was full of foreboding, the traffic lumbering along in disarray. The city clocks had already struck eight by the time our part of that sombre procession reached the prison. There was no sign of life at first. Then we glimpsed Colin, diminutive under the stone wall, fag in hand, waiting. He slid into the back of the car with hardly a murmur, except a request to stop at the nearest litter bin to dispose of his prison-issue shoes. We told him how the family were assembling in his house that day, that there were to be great festivities. There was silence nearly all the way to Stamford. Then a tentative voice began to hum in the back seat:

What can I give him, poor as I am? . . .
Yet what I can I'll give him –
Give my heart.

We had not realised it, but visiting police cells, witnessing
in court and regular trips to prison were equipping Margaret
and me for part of our book van ministry. We had already
received an invitation to visit the local Langley House Trust
home at Wing Grange. Here were men who were still
recovering from what prison had done to them and their
families. Some of them were deeply distressed, because
parents, wife or girl-friend had not been able to stand all the
implications and indignities of that Visits Room and no
longer wished to receive their men back. For them, Wing
Grange was home. Our first visit there was on a wet
November evening. The young girl who answered the door
looked bewildered.

"Good News Van? Hang on. I'll go and ask. You'd better
wait in the kitchen."

Blessedly, the kitchen was warmed by an institution-sized
Aga. We rested our load of books on the table and waited.
Soon a youngish man strode through, on his way to a
scullery. "What's this? Another jumble sale?" he smiled.

"No. It's Christian books."

He strode dismissively on his way.

"For free!" I called hopefully. "It's a library."

"Free? Oh well, now, let's have a look." Eddie was to
become one of our regulars. He brought in several more of
his friends who had been whiling the evening away in the
television room. Not all of them could benefit from our
books. Some were not interested; some could not focus their
eyes properly because of medication they were receiving;
some had never learned to read; but they all enjoyed the
company and were soon exchanging jokes, news and,
eventually, confidences. My experience with Colin had
made it all too clear just how cut off from ordinary life and
how condemned these men had felt during years of
imprisonment.

Margaret and I had been invited to speak about the work of the Good News Van at the Torch Trust in Hallaton, near Uppingham. We had discovered that they, many of them blind themselves, produce not only braille books but also spoken tapes for the use of blind people. As a result of our concern for those we knew who were handicapped by partial sight, stroke, Parkinson's disease or muscular dystrophy, we had obtained permission to use the Torch Trust tapes for these people, as well as for the blind. Now we could lend them at Wing Grange, once the men there had a tape-recorder.

A new resident, Bob, arrived from Birmingham Prison. He talked with us freely and confidently straight away, declaring that he wanted three favours from us: first, the address of Alcoholics Anonymous; second, confession and Mass from a Roman Catholic priest; third, our appreciation of his new second-hand size-ten shoes. Bob did not realise it, but he was to open the way for new work for us. On his behalf, I telephoned the Roman Catholic priest for Bob's district, Oakham. He promised that he would call and see Bob. Then he paused. "Why are you involved with Wing Grange, Mrs Allan?"

I explained briefly what we did when we visited with the Good News Van.

"Why ever don't you come to Ashwell? It's an open prison. They'd be delighted to have access to lively Christian books. Do you have some taboo on prisons? I'm R.C. Chaplain there."

"No. But we only come where we're invited."

"How can they know there's the possibility? You must write to the governor, if you're willing, offering your services. He'll pass the letter on to the other chaplains and to me and then, hey presto, you're away!"

I wrote, full of high hope, but received no answer. Christmas was coming. I wrote again, this time explaining that our sole wish was to reach the prisoners with Christian books, especially at Christmas, when many would be feeling sore that the festival was going on in the world outside, oblivious to them. Then I telephoned the Governor. The letters had been passed by him to the relevant authorities, but little could now be accomplished that side of Christmas by way of a visit. We went to see the Governor and he accepted a tiny supply of books to be set out on display for loan in the prison chapel. Soon after Christmas we were in, again in a Visits Room, but in a different guise. This time we were to meet men in a very different situation from that of Colin. Some were there for long stretches, but we were not at first to know the nature of their crimes, nor the nature of their family problems. These men did not fraternise with each other easily; but once they knew that a fellow-prisoner had read and enjoyed the same book as they, a link was forged. Gradually they opened up, not only to one another without back-biting and suspicion, but also to us. Discussion of books grew into discussion of mutual problems in relation to belief: belief at first in any power or God; gradually to an admission of a tentative belief in the God of the Bible and eventually to commitment to Jesus Christ. We were warned that several of these men were in for fraud and deception, that we were not to take their commitment too seriously.

However, as the years passed and one inmate lent books all round his block, a camaraderie developed.

We arrived in Easter week, two or three years later. The men were still elated from Easter Day. They had not been asked, as was customary, to sit apart from the rest of the congregation in a nearby church. In fact, one had been asked to read the lesson. They were particularly radiant because their little prayer group – two or three men who now met in the block regularly – had heard glad news:

"Did we tell you about the screw's wife, Pauline? The one who had cancer? Wasn't expected to live? She's completely healed! Discharged from hospital! How about *that*?"

We sat down and read at their request, not just from any Christian book, but part of the Gospel for Easter:

"A week later, the disciples were together again indoors... *The doors were locked*, but Jesus came and stood among them and said, 'Peace be with you'." (John 20:26).

17. Flames of Faith

The tea trolley was being wheeled into the tiny room behind the Baptist Chapel. Someone was totting up the loose coins accumulated on a plate as collection.

"Now, ladies, I'm sure we all want to thank these girls for coming and giving us such an interesting talk..."

A walking stick clattered to the ground; chairs were pushed back; a cup of tea was thrust into my hand; there were urgent exchanges about lifts and local bus times, enquiries about health and hearing aids: the elderly could at least go home to their own hearths, glad to have seen their friends, glad to shift position, glad to get away.

Joan, the motherly middle-aged lady who had invited Margaret and me to speak about our work, gave me a warm hug. "Isn't it all exciting!" An envelope containing "petrol expenses" slid into my hand. "As you can tell, some of these ladies are past caring much about trying to see small print, let alone to concentrate on a fat book. But they love seeing you young things and hearing what the Lord's doing. But some of them would love to have a regular borrow – and I know my daughter, Julia, would be happy to have a book morning in her village. She's got lots of young friends, mums and children. Worth doing, if you can spare the time?"

Julia lived in Cottesmore, in another part of the village from the R.A.F. station where we were already becoming regular visitors. Her house was in smart contrast to the worn brown chapel room where we had met her mother. We unloaded our plastic baskets of books from their stacks on the shopping trolleys onto a table in a spacious living area. This stretched the width of the rear of the house. A poodle pup attended our activities and was swiftly banished to the patio, relegated to ignominy beyond sliding French windows. As we sipped Julia's real coffee I began to notice the details which made the whole visit so welcoming. Julia herself, elegant and alert, was concerned about our personal well-being as well as about the books. Every time the door-bell rang as yet another friend arrived, the pup barked and Julia sparkled with delight. All sorts of people assembled round that table and each was treated as a particularly special person. That was a vivid illustration for me of what Jesus' love for each of us is like.

Brenda came; familiar with many of our books, she was looking for one that would refresh her own soul without making too many immediate demands. She came across Rita Nightingale's *Freed for Life*, which she had not seen before, and which as it is located in Thailand, certainly made no direct demands on her. Yet it did have some relevance to her own experience. Her husband was away abroad most of the year, in a secular job, just as Rita Nightingale had been when she was so suddenly thrust in prison.

Someone who worked at a nearby school needed to borrow for a friend going through the stress of divorce. She herself needed to understand what this experience could be like and eventually borrowed *No Pit too Deep* by A. Fordham and *Prayer without Pretending* by Anne Townsend for the benefit of both her friend and herself.

Some were returning books borrowed at the Baptist Chapel, and we learned plenty about their reaction to our recommendations:

"Have you got any more Catherine Marshalls? No, I've read that ... and that ... and that ... Ah, here's one come in that's new to me! It's no good your suggesting Corrie Ten Boom. I can't stand the stress."

"Haven't you got anything more for the younger teens? Mine read all C.S. Lewis's Narnia series when they were eight- and nine-year-olds. There must be lots more publications for older children surely..."

"This *God's Smuggler* is pretty dog-eared. Either very old, or very well used!"

We learned, too late, that we should spend some of the money we had been given on tough plastic book covering, before the more popular paperbacks began to look chewed round the edges.

A tall man wearing a thick naval jersey strolled into the room, hands in pockets, detached and disconsolate. He helped himself to coffee, turned over the tape which had been discreetly playing Fisherfolk music in the background and joined me. This was Julia's husband.

"What about you, Peter? Do you want a book?"

"Not at the moment, thanks. I've got lots to think about."

"Not at work today?"

"Hasn't Julia told you? They don't want me in the navy any more. Slight hearing defect – makes any man unacceptable." He shrugged. "Don't know what else to do. The navy's been my life..."

"Yes, poor darling. We're going through hard times with Peter, Ros," called Julia from the sitting room. "Can't find anything to keep mind and body active enough, can you, Peter? Any suggestions, Ros?"

"What's your particular line?" My mind was clicking off the local professions: teacher, doctor, social worker...

"Marine engineering... submarines."

"Oh," I gulped helpfully.

Brenda chipped in with some encouragement.

"You've done a lovely job, cleaning my three-piece suite, Peter. Now, cheer up! There's probably plenty more people who need carpets or furniture cleaned. Haven't you anyone in Stamford, Ros?"

I watched Peter's glum expression and knew that the whole of his life was falling apart. "It's O.K.," he reassured us all; "I'm not done for yet. Grannie had a word from the Lord for me, didn't you, Grannie?"

Julia's mother, Joan, had been settling the elderly in the armchairs among the cheese-plants at the far end of the room. She brightened at the mention of her name and bustled back among those round the book-table.

"Yes. Now let me think. I've got it written down specially for Peter. How does it go? 'And I will restore to you the years that the locust hath eaten... And ye shall eat in plenty, and be satisfied, and praise the name of the Lord your God, that hath dealth wondrously with you: and my people shall never be ashamed.' That's Joel, chapter 2, Ros, and it's for Peter. Isn't it wonderful?" She slid an arm round Peter's waist and beamed with delight.

I turned to Peter's drawn face and thought: deaf, Navy reject, living far inland, now into cleaning upholstery; ridiculous. "I don't know how the Lord proposes to restore these years, Joan. I really don't. But we must pray for Peter." We prayed: that his deafness be healed and that he find fulfilling work.

Margaret and I loaded the books into the van, baffled and concerned for the whole family. The harshness and relentlessness of life in the forces was dinned into us by the earsplitting thunder of a Tornado jet passing low over the house. There seemed no hope for anyone with even the tiniest of defects.

Our own world was different. XLU suddenly developed hiccups and a very noisy engine when we were on our way home from Oakham. There was not a house in sight. Rutland Water stretched away magnificently to our right; acres of woodland clothed the hills on our left. We freewheeled on every downward slope and in faith we started to sing:

You are Lord! You are Lord!
You are risen from the dead and
You are Lord!
You are the Mighty Mechanic-and-
You-know-far-better-than-us-just-
what's-going-on-under-the-bonnet-
And Jesus Christ is Lord!

I pressed the accelerator. "Lord, get us within sight of civilisation before we grind to a standstill." The van gathered momentum *up* the next hill! We free-wheeled down the next stretch with such alacrity that it seemed a shame to stop and telephone for help. After all, the Lord could look after what he was using. The engine roared, but did not falter, until the final downhill stretch. It puttered to a triumphant standstill outside our house.

The rest was simple: lunch, a quick phone-call, and the van had been conveniently free-wheeled yet further down the hill to have its insides investigated by the local garage.

Since we had first started out, invitations to visit monthly in different towns and villages had multiplied (and we visited only by invitation). But I was still being nagged by the Holy Spirit to follow up two introductory calls we had made when we first began: one to the Earl of Ancaster's agent, enquiring about possible visits to isolated cottages on the Grimsthorpe Estate; the other to the Rural Dean of a large area to the north-east of us. One evening I rang them both and apologised for my dilatoriness.

"When you're ready," came the agent's answer, "I'm willing to pave the way anywhere with the local clergy and the villagers on the estate."

The answer from the Rural Dean:

"I've got you billed to speak to the Deanery Synod in May."

I pictured a great semicircle of dog-collars and large grins, welcoming the van into many new places.

"But, Lord," I argued as I climbed into bed that evening, "there's only the two of us. We're only human. I've got to have time for my husband, and for Juliet, Rupert and Bridget. Margaret's got her son, Andrew – and her mother. How can we fit any more in?" I pulled the blankets over my head. "It's your van. You get on with it!"

Next day was Thursday. The Ark was closed. I had already realised that, since John's appointment, there was less and less need for me to go there in the afternoons quite as regularly as I had. On Thursdays I was free of van visits, free to do the housework, the mending, the ironing ... the phone rang. It was Anne, from the town of Bourne, thirteen miles away to the north-east, the girl who had brought the Holiday Club to see the Lockerstore.

"You know that Patsy and I meet together for prayer? We've been praying for Margaret and you lately and the same words have come to us both."

"Don't tell us we're doing too much, *please*. We know it," I groaned.

"Listen to this, will you, and shut up! Patsy had it, too. 'How can they believe if they have not heard the message? And how can the message be proclaimed if the messengers are not sent out?' I know that we're supposed to help you in the Good News Van work. Can we borrow the van when you're not using it? Not in the afternoons, please, because I'm at work."

I was astonished that God had taken complete charge of the van problem so immediately. But Anne could not borrow the van at the same time as we were using it. We had been given a lump sum towards maintenance of little XLU. Could we have the faith to use that on a second van and just trust the Lord to maintain both vans his way? However, when I asked Margaret about it she was totally at ease on the matter: "We've had to trust the Lord all along for what goes on inside our XLU. Why ever start hoarding now? If we do, the Lord will abrogate all responsibility and leave us to be entirely in charge. Let's trust him!" So Patsy and Anne were to have a van of their own. Again we consulted the local newspaper for white mini-vans. There was only one van and it was sandy gold.

"That's no good." I dismissed the whole idea, fast. "It has to be white."

"Are you absolutely sure?" asked Margaret thoughtfully.

It took us both a long time to realise that the vans could be all the colours of the rainbow and still fulfil the purpose of the original dream; moreover there had been a rainbow on the side of the white van in that dream.

Still doubting, we asked Anne to share with Patsy what we had been thinking.

"That's extraordinary!" wondered Patsy. At about the same time as we had been reading the 'Motor Sales' column she had been taking a nap. "I saw an odd sight. Coming down a busy high road was a very unusual contraption. It was white at the front, but the back half was a sort of gold. I've never seen anything like it. And coming along in front was a big horse..."

Margaret and I prayed about this and decided that we really must go along and at least see the sandy gold van. However, I had misgivings. "Lord, show us whether what we're doing is faithful and true to your will and the dream you gave me." We were studying Revelation at the time. I opened my Bible to see what the next part of the chapter was all about. It was headed:

"The Rider on the White Horse," and continued:

"Then I saw heaven open and there was a white horse. Its rider is called Faithful and True..."

By the next day, the van was ours. We knew that XLU was now in good trim and very reliable and so it seemed right to give the new team that van. We could far more easily check anything wrong with the sandy-gold one since it had been sold locally.

"When we've talked about our blue and white van watering the deserts of people's lives, we've had all sorts of encouragement; but it's been unfortunate when our supporters then talk about flames of faith..." remarked Margaret drily.

"Let's paint this one with red writing – red on sandy gold. This one's for rekindling those guttering flames of faith!" By now I was feeling much braver about travelling in something bright and bold. "The white van can go off into the fens, to water them..."

We sighed with relief at the thought that we were at last going to be able to read more of the books we lent, and be free for those who needed more time-consuming ministry.

As the van returned month by month, our friendships grew deeper. People began to share more and more of their personal lives with us: their joys, anxieties, hopes, illnesses and aggravations. Some people needed prayer, some informal counselling; some, like Peter, just the continuing love and support of Christian friends. The lord was to do exciting things in the lives of Julia and Peter, but not before many months had passed.

18. The Cross of Light

The telephone rang. It was Eileen, someone we were due to visit in the book van the next day.

"You are coming to visit us in Edith Weston tomorrow morning, aren't you? Do you think you could turn up at least half an hour early? I have something rather important I need to discuss with you."

Eileen was somewhat reticent when we visited her with books. I never felt confident that I was offering her the kind of book she wanted. Now I began to fear that we were perhaps due for a sharp rebuke because we had suggested something entirely inappropriate.

We were offered coffee in Eileen's sitting-room. Nothing much was said at first, except the usual exchanges about sugar and milk. There was an embarrassed pause and then Eileen cleared her throat.

"I wouldn't have asked you to come early like this had it not been for two things. The second was so shattering that I was glad I was seated when I heard it. Otherwise I would have fallen. But I'll begin with the first.

"Do you remember, Ros, when I asked about the Christian Families Conference in Canterbury? You told me how Jean Darnall had pictured you as servants at God's heavenly banquet. Well, that rang bells for me, way back to my childhood.

"My father died when I was very small. In fact, I hardly remember him. I grumbled to my mother one day. All my friends were showing off about the things they did with their daddies.

"'I haven't got a daddy,' I complained.

'You've got your heavenly Father.'

'You can't talk to him.'

'You talk to Him when you say your prayers.'

"Later, I asked how God answered.

'He answers in ways you may not recognise – through pictures, stories, your friends – ask him to answer you.'

"That night I did. I asked God to answer me! 'I've been talking to you all the time and you haven't answered yet.'

"And there, standing on a green hillside dotted with white stones was Jesus. I tried to speak, but all that came was gibberish. However, Jesus answered me in gibberish. 'It's a game,' I thought. I followed him up the hill eagerly. We continued our conversation in gibberish. Very soon we came to a big building and went in. There was one enormous table the length of it. Lots of happy people were sitting there.

'Ooh! a banquet!' I had heard the word only a few days before in a story and I was thrilled actually to attend one. Then he spoke, in English.

'Eileen, I want you to bring the food.'

'But I'm only three,' I protested, knowing that I couldn't carry heavy trays of food.

'Start over there.'

'But I can't see anyone else doing it.'

'Yes – look, over there, there are two people.'

'Then they don't need me.'

'Start further down.'

'But I can't start all by myself.'

'You start where I said. I'll be with you to help you.'

"So I did. Almost immediately, first one came to help, then another. I could move on elsewhere. It was wonderful. Although I had seen no one outside the Hall, people were coming, one by one, until there were thousand upon thousand.

'Where do all these people come from?' I asked.

'They come from the stones you saw on the hillside.'"

Eileen paused. "I'm afraid it's rather a long story. But you see why I had to tell you. Do you mind bearing with me a little longer? You see, there's quite a bit more.

"When I was about sixteen – it must have been then, because I remember I had started my A levels a year early – I had another dream.

"This time I was standing with an after-service group of the congregation outside our Baptist church at Billingham. Have you heard of it? It's a town in Teesside, near Middlesbrough. Someone called across to me:

'You were in the van with the Good News, weren't you, Eileen?' I thought they meant 'vanguard' at the time and so I answered, 'No, I didn't start it.'

'Well, who did start it, then? I thought you had.'

'The Holy Spirit started it,' interjected a bystander.

"Then I heard myself mentioning a rather flowery Christian name beginning with R, and then I said,

'It was R – Lake and Margaret. They lived in the Midlands. And I didn't start till later. I began on a bike.'

'That's right, about thirty miles south of the first two, you were at –' and here they named somewhere beginning with 'B' and having an 'a' in it.

'Wasn't your van blue?'

'No, that was my father's. I didn't have a blue van till much later, in Yorkshire.'

"That was the end of that bit. The thing that shattered me was that I was in the Ark coffee bar only last week and they were talking about 'Ros's mum'.

'Hasn't she got a name of her own?' someone asked.

'Oh, well, yes. She's Mrs Lake.' Lake must have been your maiden name.

'Do you see? So I think I'm to be involved in what you're doing. The only place I could think of, beginning with 'B' and with an 'a' in it, is Bamburgh and that's north of Billingham. I don't really know how I'm involved yet. I haven't even passed my driving test."

Eileen had finished. I reached for my coffee cup, awestruck especially that God had fore-ordained what we were now doing, even using my maiden name when Eileen was given her vision all those years earlier and I was still

single. Obviously Eileen was to join us as servants at the
Banquet.

"You'd better get on with your driving test," I remarked
flatly. Best not to get too excited yet.

*   *   *

Soon after that, Margaret and I were invited to speak at a
Ladies' Meeting at the nearby small town of Market
Deeping. I was driving, searching in my memory for the
directions we had been given. Suddenly I saw instead a light,
diffuse and pure like that at the place where a rainbow
touches the earth. That light started in Stamford and spread
far into the north and similarly deep into the south, across
the Channel and into Europe. As it went east across East
Anglia and over the sea and west through Wales, I
recognised the form of a great cross.

I knew that, whatever else I said at the Ladies' Meeting,
that cross had to be described. And I was to tell about it
wherever we went in the course of that week, on van visits.

However, another shadow had fallen almost imperceptibly on my personal life. A tiny spot had developed on my
shoulder. Aggravated by continual rubbing from my bra
strap, it had grown bigger and redder. It refused to heal.
Margaret was concerned when I showed it to her and
suggested I consult my doctor. I was referred to a skin
specialist, I assumed because it was unsightly and rather a
nuisance. The specialist, to my disconcertment, remarked
that there were several more lesions across my back and
offered to remove them all, there and then, under local
anaesthetic. I was pleased, since there would be an end to my
problems with the spot on my shoulder. However, almost
immediately afterwards I received a letter: since there was
definite laboratory evidence that the lesions had not been
completely removed, it would be advisable for me to return
soon. I looked at the date for the appointment: during the
very week when I received the letter.

Gradually I realised the implications of this. The specialist was concerned for the early removal of the remains of the lesions. I wondered about the future. Was it skin cancer? How, exactly, did that affect people? What precisely was the extent of the danger? What possible cures were there? It was difficult to discover the answers.

I had been reading Francis McNutt's book, *Healing*. There were many factors that could possibly account for people not being healed of sickness and disease. One which stood out for me was the need for forgiveness, all ways round: forgiveness of us by our heavenly Father; forgiveness of us by others; our forgiveness of other people. Jesus' only comment on the Lord's Prayer is:

"If you forgive others the wrongs they have done to you, your Father in heaven will also forgive you. But if you do not forgive others, then your Father will not forgive the wrongs you have done."

It was time for me to investigate my life and make sure the channels were free between my heavenly Father and me. I knew that I had somehow to make a fresh start with a family relationship which had been wrong for years. An acquaintance of my parents had hurt them grievously and as a result I had made little or no attempt to relate to him. Now I had to "forgive" in whatever way I could in the circumstances. The outcome of much prayer and embarrassed cogitation was a long friendly letter which I sent off before my appointment with the specialist. An interesting side-result of that is that the newly reconciled friend has come to live very near . . .

I also had to think carefully through a painful relationship where I had offended by starting work in the Good News Van. That required a genuine apology from me for the hurt this had somehow, inexplicably caused. After all, I was still buzzing around in the van, even telling about the cross of light; but a friendship had been marred and I was required to do all within my power to seek forgiveness for whatever wound I had caused, however inadvertently.

Before the hospital appointment, I felt the urgent need for someone to pray for my healing. I was in the Ark coffee bar and so I grabbed the first two committed Christian friends I knew. We all trooped down to the quiet room, where I explained the situation to a mystified Jean and Elizabeth. Quietly and confidently they laid hands on my shoulders and back. As they prayed, I felt a sharp tingling in four or five places on my back. I knew that the Lord was at work. It was all very brief and matter-of-fact.

Then I went to see the specialist. He had with him a student. He consulted my file.

"Ah now, Mrs Allan. How is the shoulder?" Then, to the student: "You will see . . . that this particular lesion is completely healed . . . but round the back here, you will see . . . oh . . . well, perhaps over here . . . oh . . ." He cleared his throat, mystified. "You may put your jersey back on, Mrs Allan. We'd like you to come back in three months' time."

I was to return annually for the subsequent five years, but, so far, I have received the same dismissal.

More immediately there were to be results with the Good News Van service. On the Friday evening of that week of rainbow-talk and healing the telephone rang.

"My name is David Smith and I live in Donington. We have seen an article about your work in the Rural Evangelism newspaper. It links in with a call my wife, Ruth, had of a very similar nature. We'd like to know a lot more about your work and start a similar library ministry around here." Overjoyed, I returned to dishing up supper.

Again the telephone rang.

"Do you remember when you came with the books to Stoke Dry last Tuesday? Well, Sally and I both heard you tell of the cross of light you'd seen when you were on your way to Market Deeping. We knew we were being challenged to start a van ministry around here. Can we talk with you more?"

Two possible new van teams in one week.

David, the first caller, was a Pentecostal pastor. Did this make any difference to his willingness to encourage people he visited to continue wholeheartedly in the local church where they belonged? He had said that he was keen for every Christian to be strengthened where they were. However, when Tony Gough came with us to meet David and Ruth, I noticed that he was dressed in clerical black and looking very Anglican. I was concerned lest there should be a denominational undercurrent to the conversation. We arrived at the drive gate. Tony leapt out to open it for the van to pass through. As he did so, his clerical collar pinged off his neck. With great presence of mind, and rueful wink, he hung it on the gate-post. The Good News work remained inter-denominational.

Two vans, both blue, were provided for these teams. Both teams had the idea of streams of living water watering the desert as a symbol of their Christian ministry.

Mention of the cross of light at the Deeping ladies' meeting had begun to bear fruit there. During the ensuing weeks, Felicity, one of the ladies present on that occasion, had enquired about baptism in the Holy Spirit. I had got to know her well as a friend. Eventually, she asked to receive the baptism for herself. She had grown to know and love the Lord as the result of the care of her close friend, Joan. Soon, both Joan and Felicity were eager to start a Good News Van in their area. The arms of the cross were already spreading: north to Donington, west in Leicestershire, east through Market Deeping...

And what of Eileen? She telephoned to say that she had failed her driving test yet again. She had taken it several times and was very disappointed. She had one more test to take before she moved.

"Moving? Wherever to?" I asked, dismayed.

"Hamish, my husband, has his R.A.F. posting. We're not quite sure where it's to be, but it's very soon."

"You know, if you weren't moving, I'd almost suggest you started a book ministry on a bicycle," I offered, lamely.

"Ros, have you no memory? I did tell you that in the dream I began on a bike." Eileen sounded icily impatient, and also very weary of the whole business of learning to drive.

It was only a few days later that she telephoned again, this time with a new note of excitement in her voice. "We've heard about the posting, Ros... We're to go to R.A.F. Brampton. Does that ring any bells? It's thirty miles south of Stamford down the A.1."

" – and it begins with a 'B' and has an 'a' in it!" I shouted.

We had been given enough money, gradually, over the months, for the purchase of all the other vans. Now what of Eileen's vehicle? She had to start "on a bike", at Support Command Headquarters. Hamish was embarking on further responsible work and we knew that Eileen should be given something worthy of her Lord, smart and efficient.

When I first suggested a bright red Honda Silver Stream moped, I was disappointed that she did not accept the idea gladly.

"Red for Post Office vans; red for news – Good News?" I proposed.

"Red is the colour for my star sign. No thanks. None of that."

"Not red. Why not silver? A silver Silver Stream – streams of Living Water?" Eileen's gear was silver and blue; her blue helmet happened to have a rainbow painted on it. Her vehicle registration DEW.

The cross was spreading; the streams were beginning to flow.

19. The Coming of the Wind

As we grew to know Eileen better, we learned more about her dreams. Eileen read the story of the I-Why bird when she was about eight. This bird, an ibis, took the child hero of the story on many adventures.

"I grew wistful," explained Eileen, "and told Jesus about it one night, while I was staying at my aunt's. 'It would be lovely if I could go on adventures with the I-Why bird...'

"There was a quiet rustle of feathers and an enormous white bird was in the room. He had dignity and authority.

'If you want to come with me, get up.'

"He led me through the back of the fireplace, out into the night. I expected to see the lights of Middlesbrough, but there was no sign of them.

'Jump up, then. No, not on to my back. You may ride on my wings.'

'Where are we going?'

'To Fenland.'

'Oh, over the sea to Finland!' The budding geographer in me was revelling in this.

'I said Fenland and I meant Fenland. We are not going over the sea. We'll be stopping first in Amstdorf.'

"I was puzzled. 'But wouldn't that be somewhere in Holland, with a name like that?'

'You'll see. We're taking the wind to Fenland.'

'Ooh! This feels like Diamond in *The Back of the North wind*. Are you the North wind?'

'No.'

'The west wind? – the wild west wind? That would be fun!'

'No. I am The Wind.'

"I was burrowing into the feathers on the snowy back of the ibis. 'You've got a tiny little brown feather here,' I challenged.

'Yes, usually I take the form of an eagle. But you asked for an ibis and that's what you've got.'

"We swooped down over Amstdorf. (By the way, have you understood the anagram?) There was a big merry-go-round there. I stopped and played with the big children for quite a long time. It was great fun.

"But eventually we took off again. Soon we came to an expanse of marshland veiled in cloud. The patches of this vary in colour according to their density: some were whitish, others light fawn, grey, brown and even black. As the I-Why bird flew over, The Wind came in all its force. Almost immediately, the white patches cleared. Beneath me, as the cloud vanished, the landscape assumed vivid colours. The crops began to toss in the breeze and so to dry out, ready for harvesting; the great sails of a windmill creaked into action; a farmer came from his house dressed ready to start work; a woman emerged, carrying an enormous basket of washing, which she pegged on the line, to billow dry in the wind; best of all, a little girl came running across the lawn and pirouetted a welcome to the sun. It was beautiful.

"As the wind cleared more and more of the cloud patches, the same sort of new life sprang into action. I met a girl who became a friend; we chatted for hours; her name was Rosemary (Eileen's eventual van team at Godmanchester included a girl called Rosemary).

"We often flew back to Amstdorf to play on the merry-go-round. Then, one day, I went there and it was all rather desolate.

'Where have all the big children gone?' I asked.

'They're off and away, hang-gliding.'

'What's that?'

'It's very dangerous. Never you mind, at the moment.'

"You do realise, don't you, that you are the big children and Amstdorf is Stamford?

"That was the end of that dream. Much later, when I was

fourteen and feeling rather forlorn I asked to go again. This time the I-Why bird was clearly Jesus. He said, 'No. You've grown now and can't fly on me. You'll have to grow up enough to be a child and then you'll fly with me.' Now I'm born again and am his child; I'm 'flying with the I-Why bird' in the good News Van."

Certainly the I-Why bird, or the wind of the Holy Spirit, was clearing away mists through the Christian book service in our van as well as in Eileen's. As people met together over the books in one village they began to see that here were matters which really affected their lives; they realised how important the Bible was as an authority and a point of reference in their discussions. They asked to meet together more frequently than once a month. So Margaret and I found ourselves going weekly to first one, and then two village groups, for regular Bible study. In another village books about spiritual and physical healing provoked comments:

"Talking of prayer for healing, you can all think of my Aunt Millie next week. She's got a funny lump just here and she thinks she must see a doctor..."

Next van visit:

"Thank you for your prayers last month. The lump was only a swollen tendon. But please think of me, when you say your prayers tonight. I've got an interview for a job on Monday."

Next van visit:

"I've got the job, thank the Lord. Starting on Wednesday. Joan, over there, has just told me she has a fierce headache. She'd like prayer. Can we all lay hands on her right now?"

I saw The Wind clearing away mists of Biblical ignorance, fogs of doubt and despair, dark fears of incurable illness, cloud barriers of denominational differences amongst God's people. Even black areas where evil had reigned, in the form of spiritism, witchcraft, seances or fortune-telling, were being cleared as people read books like Doreen Irvine's *From Witchcraft to Christ* or Trevor Dearing's *Exit the Devil*, and asked for counselling, prayer and advice. New life was burgeoning wherever the Holy Spirit moved.

People around me in Stamford were changing. The attitude of the Ark towards the van ministry was changing too. It had at first been one of suspicion, then polite indifference; now there was increasing support! I was still helping in the office from time to time. A girl who had first come in asking for me because she was in great distress over a drug addict friend, shouted across the street one day,

"I'm keeping it, Ros!" She was grinning in brave delight.

"Keeping what?"

"The baby, of course."

I had not known she was expecting a baby, let alone that she had been tempted to have an abortion. Life was going to be rough for both of them, as I was to find out later; but that young mum was eventually able to reach out with laughter, love and always with hope, to others in similar or worse conditions. The book, *The Warm Fuzzies*, was handed around among all her friends and was a symbol of her whole attitude to life. The Holy Spirit was lighting her and those she met, with love of a finer kind than they had ever found before.

Then one day someone special in a different way came into the shop. I was up in the office.

"Ros! Can you come down and help? There's someone here wants a commentary on the Psalms and I can't find it."

As I ran down the stairs a voice inside me said, "I want you to get to know this customer personally."

The only person in the shop had her back to me. She was dressed in black to the tips of her toes. As she turned, I was struck by the sadness of her eyes. The commentary she wanted was not on the shelves and so had to be ordered. That meant that she left her visiting card with her address in a village thirteen miles away. The Lord made that part easy for me. However, the order arrived and the book was collected in my absence. I was at a loss to know what to do. One Sunday afternoon a week or two later, I was sitting by the fire, knitting and chatting with my mother. For no apparent reason, quite suddenly I knew that I was being commanded to telephone Maria, the customer who had made the order.

"Well, you'll have to do the talking, Lord . . . in the middle of a weekend, too . . ." I put my knitting down and left the room.

"I'm from the Ark –" I realised the implications and corrected myself hastily, "the Christian bookshop. I'm sorry to trouble you on a Sunday afternoon, but it has occurred to me that we now have available on free loan a whole set of commentaries on the Psalms . . ."

"But we have finished that and have moved on to a fresh subject." The voice was tired and flat. I was completely at a loss and stayed silent.

"Lord, whatever are you up to? Where do I go from here?"

There was a flicker of life now. "But never mind all that. There is something I must ask you . . ."

Here it comes, I thought: a verbal slap on the wrist for intruding.

"Would you like to come and have coffee with me one morning? We can perhaps together read a Psalm of praise."

My heart leapt up in a spontaneous internal song of thanksgiving.

"Well, I should think I could just about manage that."

Over the next few months we drank coffee, we talked, went for walks around the village, talked again and became good friends. I discovered the source of the sadness: a deep depression caused partly by a crisis of belief and partly by family life. Tentatively I shared what had happened to me through baptism in the Holy Spirit. There were many return visits. We both loved music, foreign travel, the return to the intimacies of village life and, above all, the peace of the natural world. Gradually, through prayer, Maria's depression lifted. She became relaxed and much more positive. One day we were sitting at her kitchen table; the sun streamed in on the familiar strew of papers and coffee mugs; it highlighted the tiny bowl of flowers; all felt wholesome and right – and Maria asked to receive the full baptism of the Holy Spirit.

After that, everything changed. Just as the sun's rays

highlight and give life to whatever they warm, so the power
of the Holy Spirit brought verve into Maria's personality.
There was plenty of teasing, plenty of laughter now. We went
on all sorts of jaunts, but these were now flavoured anew
with a really compassionate concern for people and with
much joy.

Then one day Maria telephoned. "It's all very well my
enjoying this new life; but I really ought to tell my vicar,
Martin, what's happened to me. He must be wondering."

My heart sank. Anne and Patsy, in their Bourne van, had
already met Martin. He had been mildly interested in the
van's work but had suggested they visit the Methodists of his
village ... It was "their sort of thing."

"*Must* you?" I knew I could not and should not stop her;
but she was very young in this new abundant life and the
vicar's dry theology might quash all that was springing up in
her.

"Yes, I must."

"Very well, when are you going? I'll pray."

Maria told her vicar all that had happened to her. His
response was surprising: "Congratulations." They talked for
about an hour about Maria's experience. In the end she
asked,

"Now what about you?"

Maria asked permission to introduce her friend, me, from
the Ark. So one afternoon Maria and I drove up to the high
stone wall which separated the vicarage from the rest of the
village. There was a little door, labelled "Vicarage". Beyond
was a wide sweep of well-kept lawn and a long grey stone
vicarage. A series of windows scrutinised us as we walked to
the front door; I found I was praying very hard. We were
ushered into a study; the atmosphere was forbidding.

After the initial introductions, Martin forestalled further
conversation:

"Before we got any further, there are a few questions I
need to ask you: "I've heard about the Charismatic
Movement, but I find it very difficult to understand about
what you call the Baptism of the Holy Spirit. I have been

baptised and I was supposed to have been given the Holy Spirit then. There was a time in my life when people were laying hands on me every few years and praying for me to receive the Holy Spirit: when I was confirmed, when I was ordained as a deacon, then as a priest. What do I still lack? What haven't I received? Why haven't I received it? Are you saying that the church through the ages hasn't had the Holy Spirit? I can't believe that. What is the relationship between what you are talking about and the ordinary life of the Church?"

There were many more questions. At first, I had winced at the suggestion that I was involved in anything as official-sounding as the Charismatic Movement; then I started to face the challenge of each remark and think through an answer; but Martin did not pause for riposte. I began to feel like a tennis player receiving innumerable serves but having no opportunity whatsoever to return the ball.

"Lord, I can't remember what his first question was now. What do you want me to say in reply?"

"Tell him what I've done for you."

That was definitive and final. I sat back, relaxed, listening, even counting the questions...

"I think that's about the lot." Martin had come to an end.

"It was about fifteen questions, all told," I remarked. "I can't answer them all ... But, if it's any help, I could tell you what has happened to me?"

It was Martin's turn to listen; he did so with interest and frustration. We talked, explained, theorised and came to a standstill.

"Thank you for telling me and for our discussion. What do you want me to do?"

I glanced at Maria, but she did not respond. "We could pray," I offered tentatively.

Martin pushed his chair back and stood up promptly, with a glance at his watch. "Let me pray for you, too." With a friendly smile he asked the Lord to bless us all as he dismissed us.

That night I was shown just how uncomfortable both

Maria and I might have made Martin feel. Our own exultant joy might have been hard to take. Next morning I telephoned an apology.

"Not at all," was the answer. "I can see you have both received something I haven't got, a sort of crown of blessings. Please pray that I may receive it too." We did. *How* we did! Nothing seemed to be happening.

Then, one Monday evening Hugh and I were dressing to go to a Full Gospel Businessmen's dinner at which Bishop Richard Hare was speaking.

"Don't you realise that Martin and his wife might benefit from this?" came the voice inside me. "He *is*, after all, one of my bishops."

I telephoned. Martin was about to dine with a general... However, he would be very grateful if I would tape-record the talk and bring it over to him one evening soon.

Bishop Hare was amusing and witty, often at the expense of the Anglican church. As Martin listened I was full of misgiving. I noted that his long legs were doubly-crossed, tied in knots with reservations... We each stared into the middle distance. But he started to chuckle. Eventually Bishop Hare told how, after a long search he knelt among Spirit-filled people of another church altogether and asked for whatever was going. He had received the fullness of the Holy Spirit; his life had been transformed. By the end of the tape, Martin was ready to receive "whatever was going" in just the same humble abandon. Together we prayed that he should receive the baptism of the Holy Spirit and the gift of preaching. Then I left, with the suggestion that Martin should go straight upstairs to bed and tell his wife what had happened. Meanwhile I whizzed along the winding lanes to Maria. With great joy, laughter and thanksgiving we celebrated the event over a bed-time drink, before I made my way home to a delighted Hugh.

There was no news of overwhelming transformation from Martin at first. But gradually he noticed one or two differences. When Maureen, his wife, complained as she often did of a painful back, instead of recommending an osteopath, he offered to pray for healing. On the grape-vine he heard that there was concern among the villagers:

"Whatever's happened to the vicar? He's gone religious!"

To his delight, people began in a new way to enjoy his sermons. A month or two passed. Then the telephone rang. It was Martin. "Maria has suggested that you come with us all on the parish pilgrimage to Iona."

I had no desire whatsoever to travel with a coachload of strangers on such a long trip. I hardly knew Martin. I had met his wife only briefly as she brought in a tray of tea during our original interview. However, Martin foresaw no problem, assuring me that I would make new friends easily, and that it could be an enjoyable break. I was to sleep on a bunk bed in a room with three others . . . I could bring an Ark bookstall in a suitcase.

He was right. Sweeps of mountain waited, windswept around a churning sea, as we made the crossing from the mainland to Mull. Then in sudden splendour a rainbow arced down through the cloud. As we stood on deck leaning against the wind Maria twinkled at me. Things were going to happen on Iona.

We were on the island only three days. On the first day Martin told us about St Columba, about the way "he was loving to everyone, happy-faced, rejoicing in his inmost heart with the joy of the Holy Spirit." Next day he asked Maria and me to meet the rest of the party in the library and discuss with them all we knew about the baptism of the Holy Spirit. Before sunrise on the day we returned to the mainland, we assembled in the candle-lit Abbey for communion. Martin and another priest officiated. We were invited to stay behind at the sanctuary step after receiving communion, if we wished to receive a new infilling of the Holy Spirit. People went forward for communion; the first one or two returned to their seats. Then it was my turn. I waited after communion, for what felt like interminable seconds, alone. The great altar candles flickered up and down the walls as the wind came in full buffeting vigour across the sea. Then I realised the comfortable presence of a plump new friend; then more and more joined the line, until it stretched across the width of the sanctuary. We each received a "topping up" or a new baptism in the Holy Spirit.

The return journey was of course as long as our first, our suitcases as heavy, the weather bleak. But now that same Spirit who had warmed Columba had anointed many of us afresh: many of our party had become "loving to everyone, happy-faced and rejoicing in inmost heart with the joy of the Holy Spirit" – The Wind had come!

20. To the Uttermost Parts

New flames were flickering into life all across the countryside where Martin was Rural Dean. I had indeed made new friends and it was good to keep in touch with each. One big difficulty was that I could not in all fairness to the donors of our Good News Van use that for personal visiting, however pastoral. Our rusty family car ate petrol as it negotiated narrow lanes and encountered quite unexpectedly, tractors, hay-wagons, a family of partridges taking a stroll or, finest of all, a cock pheasant standing aloof, in fine plumage and white stock, like some dandified eighteenth-century clergyman.

I grew more and more concerned for these rural areas. When I was growing up in Kent the heart of the village was the church, the pub, the village shop and the school. Now very often the village church is one of many being administered by a sole incumbent living in another parish; no longer is he a familiar figure strolling down the street on parish visits; he might occasionally be glimpsed driving impersonally across the miles to bury one here, marry a couple there, attend one of several parish church councils, or be present at some diocesan sub-committee on property maintenance. The pub, once along with the shop the centre for all local gossip and concern, is often a quaint rendezvous for gourmet commuters. The shop itself is dying in the face of supermarket competition in the nearby town; even the friendly concern of the milkman is being superseded by long-life milk bought in waxed cartons. The local school has disappeared; secondary-school children are leached out of the community once and for all by the school bus. The Big

House has, as often as not, been taken over by some firm or bought by the Big Businessman with interests miles away from the village, now ostensibly his "home". Nevertheless one and all expect the vicar to do the job for which he is paid: to maintain the fabric of the church, both spiritual and material. Society has given him plumes of dignity and self-respect, but too often, like the pheasant in the lane, he must ultimately survive alone – or be shot down by despair.

However, Jean Darnall had talked of God's little battalions polishing their armour for the final Battle against the hosts of darkness, and I could see people being drawn together, both by the Good News Van visits and as a result of the pilgrimage to Iona. Martin, even more than I, was grieving over the plight of the clergy in rural parishes; but here was new hope for the Body of Christ.

There still seemed to be no solution to my transport problem. I had been borrowing Margaret's own car on many of my post-Iona visits in the countryside, but I know this could not be the final answer. Then, during a long-distance telephone call, I was brought up short:

"Never mind any more of this ordinary chat," ordered my friend. "The Lord has been telling me to give you a car."

"Good gracious. Whatever for? Why? You know we already have a family car!"

"It's not for family use. It's ... it's for your ministry – whatever that may mean – don't ask me ... But you've to have whatever fits what you are doing. Just go ahead. It will come to you. You won't have to go to it."

The last remark sounded cryptic. However, Margaret was selling her car. When I came home in it for the last time, the children told me she had telephoned and that I must get in touch with her immediately.

Within the hour a plum-red mini-car drew up on the verge outside our house. Margaret had heard about it even before it was put up for sale. The person selling it had asked to bring it to show me.

"Only one lady owner ... very low mileage ... 27,000 miles ... excellent condition," began the patter.

"But Lord, what do you think?" PCT – Praise, Confidence, Trust, on the number plate... I could see nothing of the engine because it was already dark.

"We do guarantee it... There are one or two spots of rust..."

"He sounds O.K., Lord, doesn't he?"

Then Hugh's voice called across the road.

"Is that Roger over there? Why, yes, it is! Are you in the car trade now? Splendid. Rosalind, meet Roger. I used to teach him. What he sells will be all right."

"Yes, the radio signal, Roger... O.K.... Roger. Thank you, Lord," I thought.

The car problem solved, I was free to travel anywhere on whatever I could honestly call "The Lord's business" as suggested by the donor. Only a few weeks after Iona, Maureen, Martin's wife, heard Bishop Hare's tape and she, too, knelt to receive "whatever was going". Hugh and I grew to know the family well, especially as their two children more or less matched Juliet and Rupert for age and often came to spend the day in Stamford. Gradually it became apparent that Martin was preparing to move. He was being offered one or two impressive-sounding livings, but admitted to me that, like mine, his had originally been a missionary call. He was also very interested in the Good News Book Service as a spontaneous ecumenical project and had attended several of our team meetings as volunteer treasurer.

One evening he and Maureen and I attended one of Trevor Dearing's meetings. At the time when others were going forward for healing, Martin too went forward to ask for prayer for guidance about his own future. Trevor prayed.

"I can picture a jigsaw puzzle; not a complicated one; just a few big pieces; most of them are in place. The centre piece is being fitted in now! The picture is a dove."

When we heard this I immediately recognised the dove as in some way representative of the Good News work. At the very outset of our work Dennis Rose, Trevor's fellow worker, had remarked, "I see this little van flitting like the dove of the Holy Spirit linking up one with another in peace,

good-will and fresh understanding. This work will grow and
grow until it is completely beyond your control." The work
was always way beyond our control. Now the Lord was
involving Martin in it more and more.

Later Martin was to note that he had that day seen
reviewed David Prior's book, *The Church in the Home*. This
book was to contribute a lot to our thinking. One early
summer day Maureen, Martin and I were sitting on the
vicarage lawn, chatting about a mission held recently in the
parishes. Yet more people were learning afresh about the
gifts of the Holy Spirit.

There came a point in the van ministry, too, when
Christian books could take people no further. They needed
the fellowship of other Christians and they needed to grow
together. We talked of the groups that had formed naturally
during book van visits. Interdenominational Christian
housegroups embodied much that Martin had been
concerned for during his years as a parish priest: ecumenism,
outreach, growth in prayer and Bible study, ministry one to
another, learning a deeper level of love. Such groups could
be a way of catering for Christians renewed in the Holy
Spirit, but lacking Spirit-filled fellowship in their churches.
Instead of coming out and forming House Churches which
were by definition new denominations, people could remain
in or begin to attend those that already existed, and at the
same time move on in the life of the Spirit. From such home-
based fellowships new life would with love and patience
spread into the local churches themselves.

"But what can we call these groups? Interdenominational
Christian House Groups is such a mouthful," ruminated
Martin.

Maureen tweaked idly at a weed in the grass. "Why not
call them companies?"

"That makes me think of big business; stocks and shares
and so on," I protested.

"That's it!" Martin got up from his deck-chair. "Each
person *should* have a share in it, a personal interest. The
opposite of shopping around ..." He strode indoors to find

his dictionary. "Here it is: 'company: persons associating with one; any assembly of persons; a society.' Hey, how about this? 'a sub-division of a regiment' – Isn't that what Jean Darnall's 'battalions' are?" Martin was delighted. "'Fellowship' – yes, that's right... The root of the word is from Latin *cum*, with; and *panis*, bread. Sharers in bread together. Companies. Christian Companies? No. Companies of Christians? Perfect."

"So our next job is to encourage these 'Companies'. How are we supposed to do that?" I asked. "Margaret and I are already involved in four or five weekly meetings of such groups. We can't do much more."

"We ought to pray about it."

Over the next few weeks we all did pray and think. Martin realised that his vocation to missionary work could be fulfilled through the Good News Christian Book Service. By encouraging members of companies to become active in their local congregations, he could be involved indirectly in building up local churches in many places. However, if the work was to be inter-denominational, who would pay his salary? He realised that he would have to offer himself and his future to the Lord in faith. If Martin and Maureen were no longer to continue in a parish, where were they to live? None of us knew.

I prayed and thought about our own house afresh. When we moved to Stamford after Penelope's death there were just three of us: Hugh, myself and Juliet. Yet, at my father's suggestion we had inspected and eventually bought the house advertised with nine bedrooms. It had three bathrooms and a wash-basin in each bedroom. We had been persuaded to buy partly because of the superb views, partly because we could convert the top floor into a flat and thus pay part of the mortgage with the rent. But, even when we had three children, it still seemed to be an extraordinarily large house. We had a firmly established tenant in the flat; she was a good friend.

"I suppose the flat in your house isn't ever likely to be available?" asked Martin on the telephone one day.

"Kathy move? No, I'm afraid that's very unlikely. She's been on the Council's waiting list for years, but as she's on her own and has accommodation they are in no hurry. We'll just have to go on watching and praying, to see what the Lord will do."

I began to notice afresh some of the more unusual attributes of our house. We had seen much earlier the words in the stained glass of the front door: "with God's help I shall triumph." On the door handle as we went out was a rose. We were to go forth in love. As we each returned home we entered by taking hold of a plain wooden handle inset with a cross.

One evening Kathy opened that front door and came bouncing into our kitchen. She was radiant: "I've got a council flat, Ros. At last!" She hugged me with delight. "I don't know when I'll be moving, but I know it will be soon."

Within two weeks Kathy had put up a notice in the Ark asking for spare furniture; Martin and Maureen decided to come and look over our house; we were asked to store gifts from friends of furniture for Kathy; we offered Kathy, in faith, any furniture she wanted out of the flat, including the fridge, cooker and washing machine.

Then I panicked and went upstairs to Kathy again: "Can you hold tight about taking anything of ours after all? We may need to relet the flat just as it is." If Martin and Maureen decided not to come, then we would be stupid to dismantle the flat and forego our principal means of paying our mortgage.

I went downstairs to my bedroom and felt a great weight of grief. "Wherever has your faith gone?" asked the Lord inside me.

I returned upstairs. "Take whatever you want. It's completely yours for the asking." Kathy had a visitor. They both looked at me in concern, but I could not explain my behaviour because the telephone downstairs was ringing:

"We've decided to come," said Martin. "We'd like to come to Stamford tomorrow and work out how we can all share the house." I was overwhelmed with relief. The Lord's timing had been perfect, to the minute. As Martin and Maureen looked afresh at the house they knew they could select for their family whichever bedrooms they wished. When they had decided, the reason for our buying the huge house became evident. Katie and Christopher were to have a bedroom each and the bathroom on the top floor. The spare room was to be there, too, where the kitchen had been. Martin and Maureen, Hugh and I and our three children were to have a bedroom each on the first floor; there were two bathrooms available. On the ground floor were two reception rooms, a study and the big household kitchen. Below in the basement would be a "den" for all the children and their visitors, a laundry and various store rooms.

When we had first glimpsed the Body of Christ ministering to us at Penelope's death we had not foreseen that Our Lord was going to make it so evident in so many different ways. We had been seeing it brought together across the countryside in Good News Fellowships; in the villages and on housing estates in Christian Companies; and now we could be an expression of that Body ourselves in a joint household. It was now that we all noticed afresh the carving over the porch: an owl surmounting a rose – wisdom and love. Both of these were to be essential in all our dealings henceforth.

Martin had been planning over the previous year to wind down his parish activities. He had talked with and written to his superiors. Now came the big question of the date for his official resignation. As a foretaste of the future we had arranged to go on holiday together as one big household to a relatively tiny cottage on Anglesey. Throughout the fortnight the families blended together harmoniously; we had a restful, joy-filled time, swimming, sailing, canoeing and cliff-walking. Still our house at home had to be emptied of at least half its furniture and the date for the Downs' removal fixed. Martin had suggested the tentative date of September 24th and we had pencilled it into our diaries several weeks earlier. One morning we resolved to ask the Lord to show us, without a measure of doubt, when the removal should be. Together as usual we read the lectionary passage for morning prayer:

"The Lord says, 'Can't you see what has happened to you? Before you started to rebuild the Temple, you would go to a heap of corn expecting to find two hundred kilogrammes, but there would be only a hundred ... I sent scorching winds and hail to ruin everything you tried to grow, but still you did not repent. *Today is the twenty-fourth day of the ninth month, the day that the foundation of the Temple has been completed.* See what is going to happen from now on..." (Haggai 2:15–19)

In times gone by we had tried to do so much in our own strength, expecting the Lord to seal it with an approving tick; each time the result had been mediocre or our own efforts abortive. Now we were to be given a chance to let the Lord deal with us, his Temple, to let him rebuild his Church. The foundation, from our point of view, would have been laid by the twenty-fourth day of the ninth month. Our prayers had indeed been answered, even before we really made them. Martin wrote to the removers for September 24th, 1984.

He was to come to help me care for the well-being of our own van teams, which now numbered eight. Maureen was to become heavily involved with our own local book van, visiting not only in the Stamford area but also in the villages near her old home. Martin and I were to develop ministries of support to companies of Christians wherever they might be meeting. "Sit them down in companies and feed them yourselves," Jesus told the disciples at the feeding of the five thousand. We were to start the feeding by producing Bible Do-Its, practical Bible Studies to encourage people to become doers of the Word. We were to produce accompaniment tapes in the recording studio at the Ark. In September 1984 the Good News Trust came into existence to provide a proper legal framework within which all these activities could take place. Further enquiries were to come in from more distant parts of the country about the possibility of starting Good News vans elsewhere...

*   *   *

I had gone on visiting Peter and Julia in Cottesmore with the Stamford Good News Van. On one occasion Julia flung wide her front door and asked airily, "Had any visions of snow-capped Scottish mountain peaks, Ros?" I just winced wryly. "No, I'm serious. Do you have any ideas of a van in Scotland? You see, Peter has been taken back into the Royal Navy." Despite his ear defect Peter was virtually indispensable to the submarine section. He and his family were to be posted to Faslane, to the nuclear submarine base there. "Joan and I are pretty certain that we are meant to start a Good News Van service in Scotland."

My heart leapt up. The cross of light was spreading further north. "I wouldn't be a bit surprised," I remarked, as casually as I could. I unloaded the books thoughtfully. No, after all that has happened to me since the death of Penelope I would not be a bit surprised at anything the Almighty might do ...

The Ark bookshop can be found at

       8 St George's Street
       Stamford,
       Lincolnshire
       PE9 2BJ

Manager: John Chambers.

Further information about the Good News Vans and about
the tapes and publications offered free of charge by the Good
News Trust to Christian companies and housegroups can be
obtained from:

       The Good News Trust,
       28 Tinwell Road,
       Stamford,
       Lincolnshire
       PE9 2SD